BITCOIN AND BEYOND

Navigating the Digital Currency Revolution

Roger B. Smith

TABLE OF CONTENTS

INTRODUCTION

Introduction to Bitcoin Since its creation in 2009, bitcoin has been a groundbreaking digital currency that has changed the world of finance and captured the imagination of millions of people. Unlike other currencies, bitcoin does not exist or be administered by any central authority, e.g. governments or central banks. In this case, it works on a decentralization network of computers, which uses an innovation in Blockchain technology.

The creator of Bitcoin, a mysterious entity known as Satoshi Nakamoto, is central to its revolutionary nature. Nakamoto's whitepaper, titled "Bitcoin: A Peer-to-Peer Electronic Cash System," introduced the concept of a peer-to-peer electronic currency that could bypass intermediaries and enable secure, transparent transactions.

The blockchain, a distributed ledger that keeps track of all transactions across a huge network of computers, is the fundamental technology that powers Bitcoin. Participants cooperatively maintain this ledger, making it impervious to fraud and tampering. These transactions are secure and private thanks to cryptography.

The scarcity of Bitcoin is one of its most alluring features. Because there will never be more than 21 million Bitcoins, they are a deflationary asset. Many see Bitcoin as the digital version of gold—a store of value that can stave off inflation—due to its scarcity and decentralized character.

Bitcoin has a dual role: as a digital currency used for online and offline transactions and as a speculative investment. Its price can be very volatile, with spectacular variations, making it both thrilling and perilous for investors.

Around the world, there are many differences in the regulatory environment for Bitcoin. Governments and financial organizations have debated how to handle this new kind of money, which has resulted in a patchwork of rules and laws.

The complex world of Bitcoin is barely touched by this introduction. The chapters that follow will go into greater detail about how Bitcoin operates, its potential effects on society and finance, as well as the difficulties and opportunities it brings in a financial environment that is always changing.

Chapter 1 The Genesis of Bitcoin

A person or group using the alias Satoshi Nakamoto created Bitcoin, and its whitepaper, "Bitcoin: A Peer-to-Peer Electronic Cash System," was released in October 2008. When the open-source software for the Bitcoin network was released in January 2009, the network became formally established.

The primary driving force behind Bitcoin was to develop a decentralized digital currency that could function without the aid of middlemen like banks and run on distributed ledger technology, or blockchain. The Proof of Work consensus algorithm used by Bitcoin secures the network by having miners solve challenging math problems to validate transactions and add them to the blockchain.

The creation of Bitcoin's first block, also known as Block 0, by Satoshi Nakamoto on January 3, 2009, is regarded as the symbolic beginning of the digital currency. Since then, Bitcoin has developed into a well-known cryptocurrency and a store of value with an expanding user base and ecosystem of applications. The truth about Satoshi Nakamoto's real identity is still a mystery, which heightens the intrigue surrounding Bitcoin's origin.

1:1 The Enigma of Satoshi Nakamoto

One of the longest-lasting mysteries in the world of cryptocurrencies and technology is the identity of Satoshi Nakamoto, the creator of Bitcoin who went by the pseudonym. Here are some important details regarding Satoshi Nakamoto's mystery:

1. Pseudonymous Creator: It is thought that Satoshi Nakamoto is a pseudonym. The true identity of either a person or a group is still a mystery.

2. Satoshi Nakamoto published the Bitcoin whitepaper in 2008 and the initial Bitcoin software was made available in 2009. Around 2010–2011, this person or group

gradually stopped contacting the early Bitcoin community via email and online forums.

3. Mysterious Disappearance: By 2010–2011, Satoshi Nakamoto completely stopped communicating with the public and participating in the development of Bitcoin. Nakamoto last communicated with people in April 2011.

4. Various Theories: Several theories and assertions about Satoshi's identity have surfaced over time, but none have been unambiguously proven. Some people have proposed candidates like Nick Szabo, and Hal Finney, or organizations like the NSA, CIA, or even time travelers.

5. Respect for Privacy: Satoshi decided to maintain his anonymity out of a strong desire to protect personal information. In the Bitcoin community, the mystery surrounding Nakamoto's identity has emphasized decentralization and trustlessness.

6. Legacy: Regardless of who Nakamoto is, the invention of Bitcoin has had a significant influence on the financial and technological industries. The success and expansion of Bitcoin have been fueled by its open-source nature, which enables anyone to use, modify, and contribute to the system.

One of the longest-lasting mysteries in the tech and financial spheres, the mystery of Satoshi Nakamoto's identity still holds the attention of the cryptocurrency community and the general public.

1:2 Cryptocurrencies Are Becoming More and More Popular

In recent years, cryptocurrencies have become much more popular. The following are some important causes of this trend:

1. Wider Adoption: More people and organizations are embracing cryptocurrencies for a range of uses. Others use them for online shopping and international money transfers, while some use them for investing.

2. Financial Inclusion: Especially in areas with limited access to traditional banking, cryptocurrencies have the potential to offer financial services to those who are unbanked or underbanked.

3. Speculation: In the hope of making a sizable profit, many people invest in cryptocurrencies. Investors and traders have been drawn to the possibility of extreme price volatility.

4. Blockchain Technology: The blockchain technology that underpins cryptocurrencies has uses outside of them. Supply chain management, healthcare, and other industries have seen growth in its use.

5. Decentralised finance (DeFi) and non-fungible tokens (NFTs) are on the rise, bringing new use cases and

excitement to the cryptocurrency space and drawing a wide range of participants.

6. Institutional Interest: As a result of institutional investors and financial institutions' growing interest in cryptocurrencies, their legitimacy and acceptance have increased.

7. Global Economic Uncertainty: People are looking for alternatives due to economic uncertainty, currency depreciation, and inflation worries in some areas, and cryptocurrencies are seen as a hedge against these problems.

8. Regulatory Advances: Governments and regulatory bodies are constructing frameworks for cryptocurrencies to give them a degree of legitimacy and regulatory clarity that can promote adoption.

9. Technological Developments: Blockchain and cryptocurrency innovations have increased usability,

security, and scalability, making cryptocurrencies more useful for regular use.

10. Media Coverage: Social media discussions and extensive media coverage have helped to increase public awareness of and interest in cryptocurrencies.

While cryptocurrencies have become more well-known, it's important to remember that they are still fairly new and can be subject to significant price volatility and regulatory changes. People must do extensive research and use caution when making investments, just like with any other decision.

Chapter 2 Bitcoin Basics

Of course, these are some fundamentals about Bitcoin:
1. Describe Bitcoin: Bitcoin is a type of virtual currency. It does not have any physical backing and only exists digitally. It uses blockchain technology to run on a decentralized network of computers.

2. Blockchain: A public ledger known as the blockchain is used to store Bitcoin transactions. It is a series of blocks with transaction data in them. A network of nodes (computers) that verify and log transactions maintains this ledger.

3. Decentralisation: Unlike a government or a central bank, there is no single entity in control of Bitcoin. Its operation depends on a distributed network of nodes.

4. Ownership and Transactions: A cryptographic key pair made up of a public key (address) and a private key serves as a representation of a Bitcoin owner. The private key is used to sign transactions as evidence of ownership, and the public key is used to verify them.

5. Mining: Also known as "Proof of Work," Bitcoin mining is the process of using high-powered computers to solve challenging mathematical puzzles. For their efforts in generating new bitcoins and processing transaction fees, miners are rewarded. New blocks are added to the blockchain.

6. Limited Supply: The total number of Bitcoin coins in circulation is 21 million. The code includes this scarcity to make it deflationary.

7. Divisibility: The smallest unit of Bitcoin, known as a "satoshi," is one hundred millionth of a Bitcoin. This makes microtransactions possible.

8. Security: Because Bitcoin uses cryptographic technology, transactions are safe. However, to stop unauthorized access to your bitcoins, it's essential to keep your private keys secure.

9. Volatility: The price of bitcoin is notorious for experiencing large swings. It can be affected by several things, such as adoption, news stories, and market sentiment.

10. Use Cases: Bitcoin can be used as a store of value, a medium of exchange, and a safeguard against conventional financial systems, among other things. Additionally, some people use it for international payments.

11. Wallets: You need a digital wallet to store and manage your bitcoins. Wallets can be hardware-based (physical devices) or software-based (online or mobile).

12. Regulation: Different nations have different laws governing bitcoin. While some countries have welcomed it, others have put restrictions or bans on it.

13. Risk and Responsibility: Investing in Bitcoin entails risks, and it is the individual user's responsibility to protect their holdings and comprehend the technology.

Before getting involved with Bitcoin, it's crucial to learn and comprehend these fundamentals. You should also always use caution when working with cryptocurrencies.

2:1 How Bitcoin Works

A decentralized digital currency called Bitcoin uses a system called blockchain to function. Here is a short description of how it operates:

1. Blockchain: The blockchain is a public ledger where Bitcoin transactions are recorded. Each block in the blockchain contains a list of transactions. It is kept up by a global network of computers called nodes.

2. Wallets: A digital wallet is necessary to use Bitcoin. Your private keys, which are personal access codes that give you control over your Bitcoin, are kept in this wallet.

3. Transactions: You start a transaction when you want to send someone Bitcoin. The network is then informed of this transaction.

4. Mining: Transactions are grouped into blocks, and miners compete to validate these blocks by finding solutions to challenging mathematical puzzles. The block is added to the blockchain by the first miner to complete the puzzle, and they are both rewarded with newly created Bitcoin (block reward) and transaction fees.

5. Consensus: The network of nodes must reach a consensus to maintain the security and integrity of the blockchain. This is accomplished using a method known as Proof of Work (PoW), in which the computational power of miners is employed to secure the network.

6. Decentralisation: Because Bitcoin is decentralized, no one organization or authority has control over it. Because of this, it is immune to censorship and government meddling.

7. Limited Supply: Because there are only 21 million Bitcoins available, there is a limited supply, which drives up the price.

8. Security: Bitcoin controls the creation of new units and secures transactions using cryptographic methods. This guarantees the blockchain's immutability and integrity.

9. Ownership and Transfer: You must sign a transaction with your private key and have the recipient confirm it

using your public key to transfer ownership of Bitcoin. Security and transparency are provided by this.

10. Public and Private Keys: Your private key is kept a secret, whereas your public key is your Bitcoin address, which is known to others. You can no longer access your Bitcoin if you lose your private key.

In conclusion, Bitcoin relies on a network of miners to verify and add transactions to the blockchain, which is a decentralised ledger secured by cryptographic principles. It has grown in popularity due to its potential as a cross-border asset transfer and digital store of value.

2:2 The Role of Blockchain Technology

The use of blockchain technology is significant in many fields and has numerous applications. Here are a few crucial functions of blockchain:

1. Decentralised Ledger: Blockchain functions as an unchangeable, decentralized ledger. It makes it very challenging to change historical data because transactions are recorded chronologically and transparently.

2. Cryptocurrency: Blockchain is most famous for being the technology that underlies cryptocurrencies like Bitcoin. Peer-to-peer transactions are made possible by the creation and management of digital currencies, which are safe and transparent.

3. Smart Contracts: These self-executing contracts, in which the terms of the agreement are written directly into the code, are known as smart contracts. These contracts can be created and carried out using blockchain platforms like Ethereum, automating numerous procedures and eliminating the need for middlemen.

4. Supply Chain Management: With the help of blockchain, supply chains can track the beginnings and destinations of their products. This can improve

traceability and transparency, lowering fraud and ensuring product authenticity.

5. Voting Systems: Blockchain can be used to create safe and impenetrable voting records in electoral systems, potentially lowering electoral fraud.

6. Identity Verification: Blockchain technology can be used to securely and decentralizedly verify an individual's identity, giving people more control over their data and lowering the risk of identity theft.

7. Cross-Border Payments: By removing middlemen and shortening settlement times, blockchain has the potential to simplify and lower the cost of cross-border payments.

8. Asset tokenization: Blockchain technology can tokenize physical assets like stocks, real estate, and fine art. This makes trading and transferring ownership of these assets simpler.

9. Healthcare: Blockchain can be used to safely store and share medical records while preserving the confidentiality and integrity of patient information.

10. Notary Services: Documents can be notarized using blockchain, creating a time-stamped, tamper-proof record of crucial papers and contracts.

11. Transparency and Trust: By enabling all users to view and confirm transactions on the network, blockchain improves transparency and trust in numerous processes.

12. Immutable Data: The blockchain is a useful tool for preserving historical records and evidence because it makes it very difficult to change or delete data once it has been recorded.

13. Interoperability: Work is being done to build blockchain networks that can communicate and share information, increasing the likelihood of widespread adoption.

14. Data Security: By encrypting data with cryptographic methods, blockchain can improve data security and privacy.

15. Environmental Initiatives: As traditional Proof of Work (PoW) can be energy-intensive, some blockchains are looking into more environmentally friendly consensus mechanisms.

In general, blockchain technology has the potential to revolutionize several industries by enhancing efficiency, security, and transparency while obviating the need for middlemen in many operations. With the development of the technology, its applications continue to develop and grow.

Chapter 3 Acquiring Bitcoin

There are numerous ways to purchase Bitcoin. Here are a few typical methods for obtaining bitcoin:

1. Cryptocurrency Exchanges: Purchasing Bitcoin through a cryptocurrency exchange is the most common method. The popular exchanges Coinbase, Binance, Kraken, and Bitstamp are just a few examples. You can open an account, finish the required KYC (Know Your Customer) verification steps, and buy Bitcoin with fiat money (such as USD or EUR) or other cryptocurrencies.

2. Bitcoin ATMs: These are actual devices that let you buy Bitcoin with cash or a credit or debit card. Using websites or applications dedicated to tracking their locations, you can find Bitcoin ATMs.

3. Peer-to-Peer (P2P) Platforms: P2P sites like Paxful and LocalBitcoins link buyers and sellers. You can locate a seller who will accept your chosen method of payment and complete the transaction.

4. Cryptocurrency wallets: A few wallets, such as Exodus and Atomic Wallet, provide in-app exchanges that let you purchase Bitcoin right from the wallet.

5. Mining: The process of validating and adding transactions to the blockchain for Bitcoin is known as mining. Newly created Bitcoin is awarded to miners. However, since this is a resource-intensive and complicated process, most people won't find it useful.

6. Earning Bitcoin: Some platforms and websites provide ways to earn Bitcoin by carrying out tasks, taking surveys, or getting paid in Bitcoin when purchasing goods and services.

7. Gift Cards and Vouchers: From specific platforms that provide this service, you can buy Bitcoin using gift cards or vouchers.

8. Bitcoin Faucets: As part of marketing initiatives, some websites give away small amounts of Bitcoin for free.

Even though the sums are small, it's a way to begin using Bitcoin.

9. OTC (Over-The-Counter) Desks: Major institutions and investors use OTC desks to make sizeable Bitcoin purchases. For large trades, they offer better liquidity and more individualized service.

10. Cryptocurrency Peer Loans: On some platforms, you can borrow money in Bitcoin by pledging other cryptocurrencies as collateral.

It's important to think about things like security, fees, and regulatory compliance when buying Bitcoin. Use trustworthy platforms, store your Bitcoin in a private wallet, and be aware of any tax repercussions in your country. Furthermore, the price of Bitcoin can fluctuate greatly, so it's crucial to do your research and think carefully about your investment approach.

3:1 Setting Up a Bitcoin Wallet

If you intend to purchase, hold, or use Bitcoin, creating a wallet is a necessary step. There are numerous variations of Bitcoin wallets, each with unique features and applications. How to create a Bitcoin wallet is detailed below:

1. Select the Type of Wallet:

   - A variety of Bitcoin wallets are available, including:

   Software wallets are programs or applications that you can download and install on your computer or mobile device.

   - Web Wallets: A web browser can be used to access web-based wallets. Although they are practical, you must have faith in the supplier.

   - Hardware wallets: Hardware wallets are tangible objects made for offline, secure Bitcoin storage. They are regarded as one of the safest options.

2. Depending on the type of wallet you choose, download the software wallet, go to a web wallet provider, or buy a hardware wallet from a reputable manufacturer.

3. Construct or Configure the Wallet:

   - To configure the wallet, adhere to the setup instructions given by the wallet provider. For access, you might need to create a PIN, a username, and a password.

4. Keep Your Wallet Safe:

   - To protect the security of your wallet, take the following actions:

   - If two-factor authentication (2FA) is offered, enable it. Use a secure, one-of-a-kind password.

   - Record the recovery seed phrase for your wallet somewhere safe. If your device is harmed or lost, this is essential for recovering your wallet.

5. Obtain Bitcoin: Your wallet will give you a Bitcoin address, which is comparable to a bank account number,

so you can receive Bitcoin. By providing the sender with this address, you can receive bitcoin.

6. Send Bitcoin:

Use your wallet to enter the recipient's Bitcoin address and the desired amount to send Bitcoin.

7. Protect Your Wallet:

- Regularly back up your wallet, particularly after creating a new address or receiving money. Make sure your backup is kept in a secure location.

8. Test the Wallet: It's a good idea to test your wallet with a small transaction before depositing large amounts of Bitcoin to make sure you can send and receive them successfully.

9. Stay Current: - Keep abreast of any wallet software updates or modifications and educate yourself on the best practices for wallet security.

Keep in mind that Bitcoin transactions cannot be undone. Your Bitcoin may be lost if you are unable to access your wallet or if an unauthorized person gains access. Therefore, it's imperative to put security first and take precautions to safeguard your wallet and related private keys.

3:2 Buying Bitcoin: Exchanges and Marketplaces

You can purchase Bitcoin using marketplaces and exchanges for cryptocurrencies. These websites make it easier to buy and sell Bitcoin. An overview of how to purchase Bitcoin on these platforms is given below:

1. Decide on an Exchange or Marketplace with a Good Name:

  - Do your homework and choose a trustworthy and established cryptocurrency exchange or marketplace. Coinbase, Binance, Kraken, and Bitstamp are a few well-liked choices.

2. Register and authenticate your identity:

- Open a profile on the platform of your choice.

- Finish the Know Your Customer (KYC) verification process, which usually entails presenting identification documents to meet legal requirements.

3. Deposit Money: Add money to your account by doing so. The majority of platforms allow users to deposit money using fiat money like USD, EUR, or other cryptocurrencies. Bank transfers, credit/debit cards, and other payment options are frequently available.

4. Make a Purchase:

- Order to purchase Bitcoin after your account has been funded. Orders come in a variety of forms:

- Market Order: Purchases Bitcoin at the going rate on the market.

- Limit Order: This type of order lets you specify the price at which you want to purchase Bitcoin, and it only goes through when the market reaches that price.

5. Complete the Purchase: Following the processing of your order, the Bitcoin will be added to your exchange account.

6. Transfer Money to Your Wallet:

- It is advised to transfer the Bitcoin from the exchange to your individual Bitcoin wallet for increased security. Your private keys are under your control in this way.

7 Protect Your Account:

- To increase security, enable two-factor authentication (2FA) on your exchange account.

8. Watch the Market: - Keep an eye on any price changes in the Bitcoin market and decide when to buy or sell by your investment strategy.

9. Taxes and Compliance:

- Consider the tax repercussions of purchasing and selling bitcoin in your jurisdiction. To report taxes, keep records of your transactions.

10. Research Fees: - Become familiar with the exchange's or market's fee structure, including trading, withdrawal, and deposit fees.

It's crucial to remember that cryptocurrency markets can be extremely volatile, so you should only invest what you can afford to lose and only after doing your research. Be wary of phishing scams and fraudulent exchanges as well. Always use platforms that have a good reputation and good reviews, and double-check website URLs to make sure you're on the official page.

3:3 Earning Bitcoin through Mining

The way that new Bitcoins are produced and transactions are added to the blockchain of the cryptocurrency is through mining. Nevertheless, it's significant to note that Bitcoin mining has grown to be extremely resource-intensive and competitive, and it might not be feasible for lone miners without specialized equipment. What is the process of mining Bitcoin?

1. Mining Hardware: Application-Specific Integrated Circuits (ASICs) or Graphics Processing Units (GPUs) are specialized pieces of hardware that are required to mine Bitcoin. These gadgets were created to meet the demanding computational needs of Bitcoin mining.

2. Mining Software: Your hardware must be compatible with mining software. CGMiner and BFGMiner are two well-liked choices for mining software.

3. Join a Mining Pool: Due to the increased difficulty and competition in Bitcoin mining, the majority of lone miners join mining pools. A mining pool is created when several miners combine their computing resources, increasing their likelihood of receiving Bitcoin rewards. After the pool successfully mines a block, the rewards are distributed among the users based on their contributions.

4. Mining Process: By locating a unique number (nonce) that, when hashed with the block's data, results in a hash

that satisfies certain requirements (proof of work), miners compete to solve challenging mathematical puzzles. This procedure uses a lot of energy and computational resources.

5. Block Reward: When a miner or mining pool successfully mines a new block, they are rewarded with a certain number of newly created Bitcoins. As of my knowledge cutoff date in September 2021, this reward was 6.25 BTC per block, but it decreases approximately every four years in an event known as the "halving."
6. Transaction Fees: Users pay transaction fees to the miner in exchange for the inclusion of their transactions in the block. Depending on how congested the network is, these fees may change.

7. Verify and Broadcast: After completing the puzzle, a miner verifies the accuracy of each transaction in the block before broadcasting it. The new block is broadcast to the Bitcoin network for consensus after verification.

8. Consensus and Security: The Bitcoin network uses proof-of-work to secure the blockchain, which is done by miners. When the vast majority of miners concur that the new block is valid, consensus has been reached.

9. Iterate: Mining is a continuous process in which miners work tirelessly to crack new blocks and add them to the blockchain.

If you're thinking about mining Bitcoin, it's critical to take the following things into account:

- Prices: The costs of hardware, electricity, cooling, and maintenance are high when mining.

- Energy Consumption: Mining consumes a considerable amount of electricity. Ensure you have access to a reliable and cost-effective power source.

- Competition: As a result of the intense competition in the bitcoin mining industry, massive mining farms now predominate the landscape. It might be difficult for smaller miners to turn a profit.

- Regulation: Due to the wide variation in cryptocurrency regulations, it is important to be aware of the legal and regulatory aspects of mining in your jurisdiction.

- Continuous Learning: Mining hardware and software are always changing, so it's important to keep up with changes in the sector.

Individual miners may find it more practical to join mining pools or look into alternative methods of obtaining Bitcoin as the Bitcoin network develops.

Chapter 4 Using Bitcoin

It takes some time and thought to use Bitcoin. Understanding how to secure purchase, store, and use Bitcoin, a type of digital currency, is crucial. An introduction to using Bitcoin can be found here:

1. Install a Bitcoin wallet:

- A wallet is necessary to store your Bitcoin before you can use it. Mobile wallets, desktop wallets, hardware wallets, and web wallets are just a few of the different kinds of wallets available. In terms of security and convenience, each has unique benefits and drawbacks.

2. Buy Bitcoin:

You can purchase Bitcoin through a peer-to-peer exchange, a cryptocurrency exchange, or by earning it through the sale of goods or services. To purchase Bitcoin on an exchange, follow these steps: - Create an account on a reliable exchange website (such as Coinbase, Binance, or Kraken).

- Finish the verification process, which frequently involves confirming your identity.

- Add fiat money (such as USD or EUR) to your exchange account.

- Make a purchase order for Bitcoin.

3. Protect Your Bitcoin: After obtaining Bitcoin, move it from the exchange to your wallet. It's riskier to leave your Bitcoin on an exchange because hackers may target exchanges.

4. Employ Bitcoin

- Bitcoin can be used to pay for online purchases from merchants who accept it. Bitcoin is now widely accepted by online vendors and service providers.

- You can also use Bitcoin to send money to other people. You'll need the recipient's Bitcoin address to complete this.

You can withdraw money from or spend bitcoin at some Bitcoin ATMs and services.

5. Protect Your Private Keys: - The most significant aspect of Bitcoin ownership is your private keys. Never divulge them to anyone, and keep them safely stored. You cannot access your Bitcoin if you misplace your private keys.

6. Recognise transaction costs:

 - Fees are frequently associated with Bitcoin transactions, and the fee amount can vary depending on the network's load and the urgency of the transaction. When sending or receiving Bitcoin, be ready to pay these fees.

7. Stay Informed: Both the price of bitcoin and its technology are constantly changing. Keep up with developments and alterations in the world of cryptocurrencies.

8. Considerations for Law and Taxes:

- Using Bitcoin could have legal and tax repercussions depending on where you live. To understand your responsibilities, speak with a tax or legal expert.

9. Best Practises for Security:

- Watch out for phony websites and phishing scams. Make sure you're using reliable, secure services.

- To increase security, use two-factor authentication (2FA) for your exchange and wallet accounts.

10. Trade or Hodl: - Some people hold onto Bitcoin in the long term (HODL) in the hopes that its value will rise over time. Others actively trade it to take advantage of price swings on cryptocurrency exchanges. Recognize that trading carries some risk.
Keep in mind that the market can change quickly, and the value of Bitcoin is very unstable. Before using Bitcoin, it's important to do your homework, take into account your financial objectives, and assess your risk tolerance.

4:1 Making Transactions with Bitcoin

Sending and receiving Bitcoin is required to complete transactions. Here is a step-by-step tutorial on how to use Bitcoin for transactions:

1. Slide open wallet:

   - Ensure that your Bitcoin wallet is accessible and open. The wallet is required to send or receive Bitcoin.

2. Obtain the Bitcoin Address of the Recipient:

   - You need the recipient's Bitcoin address if you're sending Bitcoin to them. This address is a long string of letters and numbers that functions as an account number.

3. Launch the Transaction: - Look for a "send" or "withdraw" option for bitcoin in your wallet. Depending on the interface of your wallet, this might change.

4. Include Transaction Information:

- The following fields are typically present when sending Bitcoin:

- Recipient Address: Copy the recipient's Bitcoin address or type it in.

- Quantity: Indicate how much Bitcoin you want to send.

- Transaction Fee: You can specify the transaction fee amount in this optional field in some wallets. Faster confirmation times on the Bitcoin network are the result of higher fees.

5. Evaluate the Deal:
- Examine the transaction's specifics, including the recipient's address and the transaction's total, carefully. Verify again for accuracy.

6. Confirm and Send:
After reviewing the information, click "Send" or "Confirm." For security purposes, your wallet might ask

you to enter your wallet password or make use of two-factor authentication (2FA).

7. Await Verification:

  - After you start a transaction, the Bitcoin network must confirm it. As new blocks are added to the blockchain every 10 minutes or so, this process may take some time. Longer confirmation times may be the result of lower transaction fees.

8. Verify the transaction's status

  - On a website that tracks Bitcoin transactions, you can find out the status of your transaction by looking up the transaction ID (TXID). This will display the number of confirmations and whether the transaction has been confirmed.

9. Getting Bitcoin: Give the sender your Bitcoin address if you're getting Bitcoin. Give them the right address, as transactions to the incorrect address are final.

10. Security measures

- Verify the recipient address twice to prevent sending Bitcoin to the incorrect person.

- Be on the lookout for phishing scams and confirm the legitimacy of any payment requests.

- Never share your private keys with anyone, and keep them safe.

11. Maintain Records: Keeping track of your Bitcoin transactions, including dates, amounts, and transaction IDs, is a good idea. For tax reporting or dispute resolution, this may be useful.

Transaction Charges:

- Transaction fees can vary, so when sending Bitcoin, be ready to pay them. Faster confirmation times are frequently the result of higher fees, especially when the network is congested.

Keep in mind that Bitcoin transactions cannot be undone. A transaction on the blockchain cannot be reversed once it has been confirmed. Therefore, before sending Bitcoin, it's imperative to use caution and make sure the transaction details are accurate.

4:2 Bitcoin for Online and Offline Purchases

Bitcoin is a flexible type of digital currency because it can be used for both online and offline transactions. Here's how to carry out these kinds of transactions using bitcoin:

1. Online transactions

   a. Locate Businesses That Accept Bitcoin:

   - Seek out web-based merchants, services, or platforms that accept Bitcoin as a form of payment. This choice is now provided by many companies across numerous industries.

Shop on the merchant's website as you normally would, adding items to your cart or choosing the services you want to buy, just as you would with conventional payment methods.

c. Select Bitcoin as a Form of Payment:

- Choose "Bitcoin" or "Pay with Bitcoin" as your payment method during the checkout process.

d. Provide Transaction Information:

- Payment instructions for Bitcoin will be available on the merchant's website. The usual payment instructions include a QR code or a Bitcoin address.

e. Send the Payment: - Start a transaction in your Bitcoin wallet. Specify the amount to send along with the recipient's Bitcoin address. To send the payment, adhere to the wallet's directions.

f. Delivery and Confirmation:

- The merchant will process your order and send the products or services you've ordered after the Bitcoin transaction has been verified on the blockchain.

2. Online transactions:

a. Locate Stores Accepting Bitcoin:

While accepting Bitcoin offline is less common than accepting it online, some physical shops, eateries, and businesses do. You can locate them using apps or directories made specifically for finding such businesses.

b. Verify the In-Store Payment Options: Ask the cashier or staff for payment options when you enter a physical store that accepts Bitcoin. Some companies enable Bitcoin transactions with hardware or mobile payment apps.

c. Send the Money:

- Scan the merchant's QR code with your mobile Bitcoin wallet or type in their Bitcoin address. To complete the transaction, enter the payment amount.

d. Confirm Transaction: - Await the confirmation of the Bitcoin transaction. In physical transactions, waiting for multiple confirmations may be necessary during the confirmation process to reduce the possibility of double-spending

e. Obtain Products or Services:

- The merchant will give you the products or services you've ordered once the transaction has been approved. Take into account the following when using Bitcoin for offline or online purchases:

- Transaction Fees: Keep in mind that the cost of a Bitcoin transaction can change depending on the amount of network traffic. These costs might be passed on to customers by merchants.

- Price Volatility: Because Bitcoin's value is subject to large swings, it is important to be aware of possible price changes between the time of purchase and the transaction's confirmation.

- Security: Make sure your Bitcoin wallet is always secure, and use caution if you share your Bitcoin address. Use only trustworthy wallets and companies when transacting.

- Record-Keeping: Keep track of all of your Bitcoin transactions because you might need them for tax or accounting reasons.

More retailers and companies will probably start accepting Bitcoin as a form of payment both online and offline as Bitcoin adoption keeps increasing.

4:3 Bitcoin as a Global Payment Solution

For several reasons, Bitcoin has been positioned as a worldwide payment method. However, it's critical to comprehend both the benefits and drawbacks of using Bitcoin in this capacity:

Advantages:

1. Accessibility and Inclusivity: Anyone with an internet connection and a device that supports it can use Bitcoin,

making it available to people in areas with limited access to conventional banking services.

2. Borderless Transactions: Because Bitcoin is a global platform, cross-border transactions can be carried out without the need for costly currency conversions or international transfer fees.

3. Decentralisation: Since there is no single entity in charge of Bitcoin, it is immune to censorship and outside interference from governments and financial institutions.

4. Security and Transparency: The Bitcoin blockchain offers a high level of trust and accountability thanks to its transactions' security, transparency, and immutability.

5. Lower Transaction Costs: Compared to traditional financial services, bitcoin transactions frequently have lower fees, making them more affordable overall, especially for international transfers.

6. Financial Inclusion: Bitcoin can make financial services more accessible to people in underserved or unbanked areas, enabling them to take part in the global economy.

7. Speed: When using the Lightning Network or other layer-two solutions, Bitcoin transactions may be quicker than conventional international wire transfers.

Challenges:

1. Volatility: Compared to fiat currencies, bitcoin is less stable as a store of value due to its price's potential for extreme volatility. Both consumers and businesses may face difficulties as a result of this volatility.

2. Adoption: Even though more businesses are accepting Bitcoin, its use as a worldwide payment option is still limited.

3. Scalability: During times of high demand, the Bitcoin network may experience congestion, which will result in longer confirmation times and more expensive transactions. For wide adoption, this scalability issue needs to be resolved.

4. Regulatory Uncertainty: Users and businesses may find it difficult to comply with regulations because different nations' policies and regulations on Bitcoin vary.

5. Privacy Issues: Transactions made with bitcoins are pseudonymous, which means that even though they are not directly associated with individual identities, they can still be tracked. For users, this might cause privacy concerns.

6. Educational Obstacles: The adoption of Bitcoin may be hampered by the fact that many people are still unsure of how to use it.

7. Security Risks: Users are responsible for maintaining the confidentiality of their Bitcoin wallets and keys, and if they misplace them, they risk losing all of their money permanently.

For Bitcoin to succeed as a global payment solution, these issues must be resolved while also enhancing the platform's infrastructure and user interface. Bitcoin's potential to function as a global payment solution is becoming more important as adoption increases and technology advances.

Chapter 5 Investing in Bitcoin

Bitcoin investing can be a wise decision, but you must go cautiously and have a thorough awareness of the hazards. When investing in Bitcoin, keep the following considerations in mind:

1. Education: - Spend some time learning about Bitcoin before making any investments. Recognize its history, technology, and the variables that may affect its cost.

2. Hazard Evaluation: - The price volatility of Bitcoin is well-known. Expect significant price swings, so be ready for them. Make sure you invest only money you can afford to lose.

3. Diversification: - It's usually a good idea to avoid allocating all of your investing funds to a single piece of property. To spread risk, diversify the investments in your portfolio.

4. Investment Strategy: - Choose an approach to investing. Do you intend to hold Bitcoin for the long term (HODL) or are you only looking for quick profits? Your financial objectives should be in line with your approach.

5. Security: - To protect your money, pick a reliable and safe Bitcoin wallet. Wallets made of hardware are frequently regarded as the most secure choice.

6. Legality and Taxation: - Verify that investing in Bitcoin carries any legal or tax ramifications in your nation. Certain countries' tax authorities view Bitcoin as a taxable asset.

7. Timing: It can be dangerous to try to time the market. Regardless of the current price, you can invest a fixed amount of money at regular intervals by using the dollar-cost averaging (DCA) approach.

8. Market research: - Monitor news and market developments that may have an impact on Bitcoin's

price. Price changes can be significantly influenced by market sentiment.

9. Long-Term Viewpoint: The long-term prospects of Bitcoin hold significant potential. Although there are frequently short-term changes, some investors think it will eventually become a digital gold or store of value.

10. Security Precautions: - Watch out for phony websites, dubious offers, and shaky transactions. For your Bitcoin transactions and investments, pick trustworthy sites.

11. Trading versus holding: Choose between actively trading Bitcoin and holding it as a long-term investment (HODL). Trading can be dangerous and necessitates a solid understanding of market dynamics.

12. Emotional Control: - Feelings can influence snap judgments. Adhere to your investment strategy and abstain from acting out of greed or fear.

13. Regulatory Changes: - Monitor changes to the laws and regulations in your area. The market for cryptocurrencies may be impacted by changes in regulations.

14. Research and Due Diligence: Before investing, look into any new Bitcoin-related investment opportunities, such as initial coin offerings (ICOs) or alternative cryptocurrencies (altcoins).

15. Exit Technique:

- Choose an exit strategy. Knowing when to sell or cash out your Bitcoin, whether to lock in profits or in response to particular circumstances, is important.

Always keep in mind that investing in Bitcoin is risky and speculative. Making informed decisions and, if necessary, consulting financial experts are essential. Furthermore, past results do not guarantee future outcomes, so always proceed with caution and due diligence when investing in cryptocurrencies.

5:1 Bitcoin as a Store of Value

Bitcoin's use and value proposition are based on the idea that it is a "store of value," which is a term that is frequently used. Why Bitcoin is viewed as a store of value is as follows:

1. Limited Supply: The fixed supply of Bitcoin is one of the main characteristics that make it a store of value. Only 21 million Bitcoins will ever be in circulation. Traditional fiat currencies, which can be printed and devalued by governments and central banks, cannot compare to this scarcity.

2. Decentralisation: Since Bitcoin runs on a decentralized network, it is not governed by a single institution, authority, or group. Because it is not susceptible to centralized manipulation, this decentralization may help explain why it is so resilient as a store of value.

3. Immutability: Bitcoin transactions are kept on a blockchain, a public ledger. A confirmed transaction is irreversible, which means it cannot be changed or undone. Its dependability as a value store is increased by this immutability.

4. Security: Bitcoin is very secure and resistant to fraud and hacking thanks to its security features, including cryptography and consensus mechanisms like proof-of-work. Users can use techniques like using hardware wallets to secure their assets.

5. Global Recognition and Acceptance: As a type of digital currency and a store of value, Bitcoin has attained widespread recognition and acceptance. It is accepted by an increasing number of companies and people and traded on numerous exchanges.

6. Portability: Anyone with a computer and an internet connection can transfer and use Bitcoin. It is very portable and accessible as a result.

7. Bitcoin can be divided into smaller units called satoshis. Due to its divisibility, which enables flexible transactions, it can be used for both big and small purchases.

8. Hedge Against Inflation: Many Bitcoin supporters see the currency as a safeguard against inflation and financial instability. They contend that Bitcoin is resistant to the devaluation of fiat currencies because of its rarity and decentralized structure.

9. Long-Term Investment: Some institutions and investors keep Bitcoin as a long-term holding in the hopes that its value will rise over time. This "HODLing" approach is based on the conviction that Bitcoin can serve as a store of value.

It's crucial to remember that not everyone recognizes Bitcoin as a store of value. Its price volatility is cited by detractors as a barrier to its suitability as a trustworthy store of value. Furthermore, regulatory and legal issues can differ from one jurisdiction to another, affecting how people view the role that Bitcoin plays.

In the end, a person's viewpoint, risk tolerance, and investment strategy will determine whether or not they use Bitcoin as a store of value. Before using Bitcoin as a store of value or investment, it is advisable to conduct thorough research, think about your financial objectives, and take into account Bitcoin's special features.

5:2 Investment Strategies and Risks

Like any other asset, investing in Bitcoin entails a variety of risks and investment strategies. Here is a summary of some popular investment approaches and the risks involved when investing in bitcoin:

Investment Techniques:

HODL: Buy and Hold:

- Approach: Purchase Bitcoin and hold onto it for a long time, frequently with the hope that its value will rise over time.

- Risks: Because of how volatile Bitcoin's price can be, there is a chance of suffering significant short-term losses. To withstand market fluctuations, you also need a strong stomach.

Secondly, Dollar-Cost Averaging (DCA)

- Method: Regardless of Bitcoin's price, invest a set sum of money in it regularly (weekly or monthly, for example).

- Risks: DCA assists in reducing the danger of purchasing at a single, possibly unfavorable price point. However, it doesn't ensure profits, and you might pass up chances to purchase at a discount.

3. Buying:

- Approach: Actively buy and sell Bitcoin to capitalize on momentary price swings.

- Risks: Trading can be very risky and requires a lot of skill and knowledge. It is a difficult strategy due to emotional decisions, market volatility, and the possibility of losses.

4. Investing for the future:

   - Approach: Invest in Bitcoin with a long-term outlook, frequently with the expectation that it will increase over time.

   - Risks: Long-term investing exposes you to market fluctuations, legislative changes, and the potential that Bitcoin's value may not rise as anticipated.

5. Portfolio diversification and hedging:

   - Strategy: Include Bitcoin in your investment portfolio to diversify it and use it as a hedge against inflation and economic instability.

   - Risks: Your overall portfolio may suffer if Bitcoin doesn't perform as anticipated or if you invest an excessive amount in it.

Typical Risks

1. Price Volatility: Over brief time frames, the price of bitcoin can change significantly. This turbulence may result in sizable gains or losses.

2. Regulatory and Legal Risks: The legal and regulatory status of bitcoin varies by nation and is subject to change. The use and value of Bitcoin may be impacted by changes in regulations.

3. Security Risks: It's important to safeguard your Bitcoin holdings. You risk losing your investment if you misplace your private keys or fall prey to fraud.

4. A lack of consumer protections: Bitcoin transactions are final, unlike those in conventional financial systems. There may be few options available to you if you make a mistake during a transaction or are the victim of fraud.

5. Market Sentiment: Bitcoin's price is susceptible to speculative bubbles and crashes because it is affected by news, social media, and market sentiment.

6. Technology Risks: Despite the strength of Bitcoin's technology, network attacks, software bugs, and other technical problems can still affect it.

7. Lack of Regulation: While freedom may result from a lack of regulation, it can also expose investors to risks such as fraud, market manipulation, and shady service providers.

8. Psychological factors: Impulsive behavior, such as buying or selling because of fear or greed, can result from emotional decision-making and cause losses.

9. Counterparty Risks: There is a chance that third-party services, such as exchanges, could be compromised or improperly run, which could have an impact on your funds.

Before investing in Bitcoin, it's crucial to do extensive research, comprehend your risk tolerance, and take your investment goals into account. Some of these risks can be reduced by diversifying your investments, following security best practices, and keeping up with the cryptocurrency market. Additionally, consulting with financial experts or specialists in the field of cryptocurrencies can yield insightful information.

5:3 Storing and Securing Your BitcoinC

For your investment to be safe from theft, loss, and unauthorized access, it is essential to store and secure your Bitcoin. For storing and protecting your Bitcoin, follow these important steps:

1. Decide on a Secure Wallet First:

Decide on a trustworthy Bitcoin wallet. Hardware wallets, software wallets, mobile wallets, and paper wallets are just a few examples of the various wallet types. Long-term storage is typically thought to be the most secure with hardware wallets like Ledger or Trezor.

2. Back Up Your Wallet: Make copies of the private keys or recovery seeds for your wallet. Keep these backups in several safe places, like a fireproof safe, a safe deposit box, or encrypted digital storage.

3. Turn on 2-factor authentication (2FA)

- If your exchange or wallet supports 2FA, turn it on. By requiring a second verification step when accessing your Bitcoin, this adds a layer of security.

4. Employ Secure Passwords:

- Make sure the password on your wallet is strong and distinct. Avoid using passwords that are obvious or widely used. To create and store secure passwords, think about using a password manager.

5. Update and Secure Your Software: - Keep the most recent security patches installed on your wallet software. To protect yourself from malware or phishing scams, only download wallet software from reputable websites.

6. Make use of cold storage:

- For long-term Bitcoin holdings, think about using cold storage techniques. Your private keys won't ever be connected to the internet by using a hardware wallet, paper wallet, or offline computer.

7. Avoid Phishing Scams at All Costs:

- Watch out for phishing scams that attempt to trick you into disclosing your wallet or private keys. Always verify the legitimacy of email addresses and website URLs.

8. Safeguard Your Private Keys: - Prevent digital and physical threats to your private keys. Never give them to anyone and never keep them on internet-connected devices.

9. Become Knowledgeable:
   - Keep up with the most recent security threats and best practices in the world of cryptocurrencies. It's crucial to be aware of potential risks if you want to keep your Bitcoin safe.

10. Use wallets with multiple signatures.
    - Multiple private keys are needed in multi-signature wallets to approve a transaction. By dividing trust among numerous parties, this can add a layer of security.

11. Take into account a passphrase. Some wallets enable you to set a passphrase in addition to your private key. As a result, there is an additional layer of security against unauthorized access.

12. Protect your actual backups:

   - Store any paper wallets or hardware wallets you use as backups in a safe, fireproof area. Keep them from being physically harmed or stolen.

13. Do not use public WiFi:

   - Avoid using public Wi-Fi networks to access your wallet or conduct transactions because they can be less secure and open to eavesdropping.

14. Regularly Audit Your Holdings: - To make sure your Bitcoin is safe and has not been compromised, periodically check your wallet and transaction history.

15. Make an inheritance plan:

   - Take into account how, in the event of unforeseen circumstances, your Bitcoin will be transferred to your heirs. Securely record the information about your wallet and the access instructions.

Keep in mind that you are ultimately responsible for the security of your Bitcoin. To safeguard your investment, seriously consider taking these precautions. Consult with security professionals or individuals with experience in cryptocurrency security if you have any questions about your security setup.

Chapter 6 Regulatory Landscape

The regulatory environment for Bitcoin and other cryptocurrencies varies greatly from nation to nation and is ever-changing. Regulations may affect how cryptocurrencies are used, traded, and taxed. As of my most recent knowledge update in September 2021, the regulatory environment for cryptocurrencies is summarised as follows:

(1) The United States:

- Several agencies in the US are in charge of regulating cryptocurrencies. Cryptocurrency exchanges are categorized by the Financial Crimes Enforcement Network (FinCEN) as money service businesses and are therefore subject to AML and KYC regulations. The Securities and Exchange Commission (SEC) is in charge of initial coin offerings (ICOs) and regards some tokens as securities, while the Commodity Futures Trading Commission (CFTC) regulates cryptocurrencies as commodities.

2. The European Union: The fifth Anti-Money Laundering Directive, or AMLD5, was introduced by the EU and mandates more stringent AML and KYC standards for cryptocurrency exchanges and wallet providers. To regulate cryptocurrencies and digital assets, the EU is also developing a comprehensive regulatory framework known as the Markets in Crypto-Assets (MiCA).

3. China:

ICOs and cryptocurrency trading are both prohibited by China's strict regulations on cryptocurrencies. On domestic cryptocurrency exchanges, the People's Bank of China (PBOC) has also stepped up its enforcement.

4. Japan:

- To ensure consumer protection and AML compliance, Japan implemented a licensing system for cryptocurrency exchanges in 2017. Cryptocurrencies are accepted as legitimate payment methods.

5. South Korea has implemented AML and KYC requirements for cryptocurrency exchanges. ICOs (initial coin offerings) are largely prohibited.

6. India:

 - India's position on cryptocurrencies has changed over time. The Indian Supreme Court lifted a central bank ban on banks doing business with cryptocurrency businesses in March 2020. Regulations are still being created, though.

7. Russia:

 - Russia's position on cryptocurrencies is ambiguous. Although it is illegal to use cryptocurrencies as a means of payment, buying and selling them is permitted. The development of regulations governing cryptocurrency businesses.

8. Singapore: The city-state has adopted a pro-cryptocurrency stance and has established clear regulations and guidelines for businesses that deal with

cryptocurrencies, such as exchanges and payment services.

9. Canada:

- Cryptocurrencies are treated as commodities in Canada. Exchanges for cryptocurrencies must register as money service businesses and adhere to AML and KYC requirements.

10. Australia:

Australia has put in place frameworks for regulating cryptocurrency exchanges. For taxation purposes, cryptocurrencies are regarded as property.

11. The United Kingdom

- The UK Financial Conduct Authority (FCA) has mandated registration for cryptocurrency businesses and implemented AML regulations. However, the regulatory environment is evolving.

12. Africa:

- Different African nations have different cryptocurrency laws. While some nations have accepted cryptocurrencies, others have put restrictions or outright bans on them.

It's critical to remember that the regulatory environment is dynamic and subject to quick change. Regulations governing cryptocurrencies are influenced by things like technological advancements, international cooperation, and public opinion. It's crucial to stay current with local regulations and seek legal counsel when necessary if you want to deal with cryptocurrencies safely and legally.

6:1 Government Approaches to Cryptocurrency

Government responses to cryptocurrencies differ significantly between nations, reflecting a variety of regulatory stances and viewpoints. These strategies are influenced by a variety of elements, including the nation's political and economic situation, worries about the stability of the economy, and shifting attitudes toward technological advancement. Following are a few typical government responses to cryptocurrencies:

1. Proactive Regulation: Recognising the potential advantages of cryptocurrencies while attempting to reduce risks, some nations have decided to actively regulate them. They frequently take action to prevent fraud, tax evasion, and money laundering while promoting the development of the blockchain and cryptocurrency industries.

- As examples, consider Singapore, Japan, the United States, and the European Union.

2. Strict Rules and Prohibitions:
On the other hand, some governments have put in place strict guidelines or outright bans on cryptocurrencies. They frequently refer to worries about consumer risk, potential illegal use, and financial stability.

Examples include China and India.

3. The wait-and-see strategy: Many governments are adopting a circumspect "wait-and-see" strategy, watching the cryptocurrency market before enacting extensive regulations. They might consult key players in the industry and weigh the advantages and risks.

- Examples: The United States, Australia, and Canada are just a few of the nations that fall under this category. Encouragement of Innovation

- A few nations have adopted a strategy that supports blockchain and cryptocurrency innovation while offering businesses clear regulatory guidance. They seek to draw talent and cryptocurrency startups.

Examples include Estonia and Switzerland.

5. Legal Acceptance of Cryptocurrency: Governments in some areas have granted cryptocurrencies legal status by accepting them as a legitimate method of payment. These regions might have transparent tax laws governing cryptocurrency transactions.

- Japan and Germany as examples.

6. Industry Regulation:

Governments occasionally impose sector- or use-specific regulations on cryptocurrencies and blockchain technologies. Instead of a general framework, they might implement specific rules for cryptocurrency exchanges or initial coin offerings (ICOs).

Examples include South Korea and the US (SEC regulates ICOs).

7. Global Collaboration:

- Cryptocurrency laws frequently cross national boundaries. Some governments take part in international projects and forums to coordinate efforts and create unified strategies for regulating cryptocurrencies.

- Examples: The G7, G20, and Financial Action Task Force (FATF) work on international standards.

8. Taxation and Reporting: - A lot of governments tax cryptocurrency transactions and demand that people and companies disclose their cryptocurrency holdings. The purpose of these rules is to guarantee tax compliance.

- As an illustration, various nations have adopted cryptocurrency tax regulations.

9. Sandboxes for fintech:

- Regulatory sandboxes have been introduced by some governments, allowing fintech and cryptocurrency startups to test out cutting-edge technologies while benefiting from some regulatory relief. Collaboration and innovation are fostered by this.

- Singapore and the UK as examples.

10. Knowledge and Awareness

Few nations concentrate on public education and awareness campaigns to educate citizens about the advantages and risks of cryptocurrencies as well as the best practices for safe participation.

- Examples: Several nations run educational campaigns about cryptocurrencies.

The regulatory environment for cryptocurrencies is constantly changing, and new developments are frequently made. It's critical for those working in the cryptocurrency industry to stay up to date on legislative changes and to abide by local laws. Navigating the complex regulatory environment can be made easier by seeking the advice of legal specialists and business experts.

6:2 Taxation and Legal Considerations

Using, trading, and investing in digital assets all involve tax and legal ramifications that are different depending on the country. Here are some important things to think about about the legal and tax implications of cryptocurrencies:

One is taxation

- Income Tax: Since many nations treat cryptocurrencies as assets or property when you receive them in exchange for goods, services, or mining rewards, income tax may be due. Depending on how long you keep a cryptocurrency before selling it or using it, your tax obligations might change.

- Capital Gains Tax: Capital gains tax is frequently applicable if you sell or trade cryptocurrencies. Depending on how long you held the assets, either a lower or higher tax rate may apply.

- Gift and Inheritance Tax: In some jurisdictions, giving or inheriting cryptocurrencies may have tax repercussions. Understanding your local laws is crucial because rules differ from place to place.

- Reporting Requirements: For tax reporting purposes, some nations require cryptocurrency users to disclose their holdings and transactions. Penalties may be imposed for failure to report.

- Tax Deductions: In some circumstances, costs associated with cryptocurrency-related activities, like mining or trading, may be written off against your taxable income.

2. Legal Considerations:

- Regulatory Environment: Recognise how cryptocurrencies are governed in your nation. The use, trading, and investment of cryptocurrencies can all be significantly impacted by regulations.

- Know-your-customer (KYC) and anti-money laundering (AML) regulations: These laws frequently apply to cryptocurrency exchanges and businesses. When using these services, be prepared to provide identification and transaction history.

- Security and Custody: To reduce the risk of fraud and hacking, select reputable and secure cryptocurrency exchanges and wallets. Protect your private keys by following best practices.

Initial coin offerings (ICOs) and token sales are frequently the focus of regulatory oversight. To ensure that any ICO or token sale complies with local laws, do thorough research on it.

- Licencing: Some nations demand licenses from cryptocurrency businesses, including exchanges. Make sure the services you utilize have the appropriate licenses, if necessary.

- Consumer Protection: In some jurisdictions, cryptocurrency transactions are subject to consumer protection laws. Recognize your rights and options for legal action.

- AML Compliance: Businesses dealing in cryptocurrencies are frequently required to report shady transactions and adhere to AML guidelines. In some circumstances, this may lead to the freezing or seizure of assets.

- Tax Evasion: Underreporting or failing to report cryptocurrency income as income can have serious legal repercussions, such as fines and penalties.

- Cross-Border Transactions: Take into account the tax implications and legal requirements in both your home country and the recipient's country when conducting cross-border cryptocurrency transactions.

To ensure compliance with the law, it is essential to stay informed about local tax laws and regulations and seek advice from a tax expert or legal specialist. It's crucial to keep up with any legal changes that might have an impact on your cryptocurrency activities given the rapidly evolving nature of cryptocurrency regulations and the global nature of digital assets.

6:3 International Regulations and Compliance

The landscape of cryptocurrencies is complex, and international regulations and compliance are always changing. The creation of regulatory frameworks is being worked on by numerous international organizations as well as individual nations to address the problems and opportunities that cryptocurrencies present. An overview of global laws and compliance issues is provided below:

1. FATF: Financial Action Task Force

- The FATF is an intergovernmental organization that establishes international standards for countering the financing of terrorism and anti-money laundering (AML). 2019 saw the release of FATF's cryptocurrency guidelines, which obliged its members to enact AML/CFT regulations and regulate virtual asset service providers (VASPs).

2. The G20 and the G7:

International forums for economic cooperation include the Group of Seven (G7) and the Group of Twenty (G20). They discussed cryptocurrency regulations and emphasized them in statements they released.

3. The European Union (EU): The EU has been developing frameworks for cryptocurrency regulation. A comprehensive regulatory framework for digital assets in the EU is what the Markets in Crypto-Assets (MiCA) proposal seeks to establish.

4. Agreements that are bilateral and multilateral:

- To collaborate on efforts to regulate and enforce cryptocurrency, some nations have signed bilateral or multilateral agreements. For instance, the United States and several other nations cooperate and share information when looking into crimes involving cryptocurrencies.

5. National Regulations: Each nation has put in place its own rules and compliance requirements for cryptocurrencies. AML/CFT standards, reporting requirements, tax laws, and exchange licensing requirements are a few examples of these.

6. Compliance with Tax Law:

- Many nations have created tax regulations for cryptocurrencies that mandate that both individuals and businesses report their cryptocurrency holdings and transactions for taxation.

7. Transactions Across Borders:

- Regulatory compliance in both the countries of the sender and the recipient may be a requirement for international cryptocurrency transactions. Observing AML and CFT regulations may be necessary.

8. Travel Rule:

The FATF's "Travel Rule" mandates that VASPs gather and share customer information for cryptocurrency transactions that exceed a specific threshold. International transactions must adhere to this rule.

9. Exchange Rules:

- When dealing with clients from different nations, cryptocurrency exchanges frequently encounter problems with regulatory compliance. Every jurisdiction they operate in has unique regulatory requirements that they must adjust to.

10. Legal arbitrage

- Some companies and users might try to operate in areas with lax regulations to benefit from regulatory differences. Regulators are working harder than ever to eliminate these opportunities for regulatory arbitrage.

11. Global Standards and Cooperation: - Global standards and cooperation are being established for the regulation of cryptocurrencies. By doing this, regulatory fragmentation will be lessened and consistency will be created.

Businesses and individuals operating in the space need to stay informed and compliant with pertinent regulations given the rapidly evolving nature of cryptocurrency regulations. Participants in the cryptocurrency industry can help ensure compliance with international and national regulations by adhering to AML/CFT measures, taxation regulations, licensing requirements, and best practices. When necessary, seeking advice from legal professionals and regulatory bodies is advised.

Chapter 7 Beyond Bitcoin: Altcoins and Tokens

Beyond Bitcoin, the cryptocurrency landscape consists of a huge selection of alternative coins and tokens, each with its special characteristics and applications. Tokens and alternative currencies differ in the following ways:

Altcoins:

The term "Altcoin" is a combination of the words "alternative" and "coin." Any cryptocurrency other than Bitcoin is meant by this. The goal of altcoins is to offer distinct features, capabilities, or advancements over bitcoin.

2. Independent Blockchains: A lot of alternative currencies have their blockchains and aren't based on the Bitcoin blockchain. Ripple (XRP), Litecoin, Bitcoin Cash, and Ethereum are a few well-known examples of altcoins.

3. A Variety of Use Cases: Altcoins have a variety of uses, including privacy features, fast transaction confirmation, smart contracts, and alternative consensus mechanisms. For instance, while Monero focuses on privacy and anonymity, Ethereum pioneered the idea of smart contracts and decentralized applications (DApps).

4. Market Capitalization: The market for cryptocurrencies is dominated by altcoins as a whole. Some, like Ethereum, are regarded as being a significant component of the cryptocurrency ecosystem and have a sizable market capitalization.

5. Trading Pairs: On various exchanges, altcoins can be traded against bitcoin or other cryptocurrencies. Altcoins are frequently used by traders to diversify their holdings or profit from price swings.

Tokens:

1. Constructed on Pre-Existing Blockchains: Tokens are digital assets built on pre-existing blockchains like Ethereum. They create and manage assets using the

infrastructure of the blockchain. When created on the Ethereum blockchain, these are sometimes referred to as "Ethereum tokens" or "ERC-20 tokens."

2. Tokens are highly customizable and can stand in for a variety of assets, including digital goods and services as well as more conventional assets like real estate or stock in a company.

3. Utility and Security Tokens: Utility tokens and security tokens are two common categories of tokens. Security tokens, like conventional securities, represent ownership in an underlying asset, whereas utility tokens grant access to a good or service.

4. Initial Coin Offerings (ICOs) and Token Sales: Through ICOs or token sales, many tokens are created and distributed. Tokens are bought by investors in the expectation of future value growth or to gain access to a platform or service.

5. Diverse Use Cases: Tokens have a variety of uses, including enabling peer-to-peer transactions, powering decentralized applications, and representing real-world assets.

6. Regulatory Considerations: Token regulations can differ from one jurisdiction to the next. Utility tokens might be subject to a different regulatory regime than security tokens, which are frequently governed by securities laws.

7. Decentralised Finance (DeFi): Tokens that enable lending, borrowing, and decentralized trading without the need for conventional financial intermediaries have become increasingly popular in the DeFi market.

The diversity and innovation in the cryptocurrency industry are represented by altcoins and tokens. Although Bitcoin continues to be the most well-known and widely used cryptocurrency, these alternative assets provide unique features and functionalities that are tailored to different use cases and sectors. It's crucial to research the specific project, its technology, and the team behind it before investing in or using altcoins and tokens. You should also take your investment objectives and risk tolerance into account.

7:1 Introduction to Altcoins

The term "altcoins," which stands for "alternative coins," refers to all cryptocurrencies besides Bitcoin. The first cryptocurrency, Bitcoin, was developed in 2009 under the pseudonym Satoshi Nakamoto by an unidentified person or group of individuals. Since then, tens of thousands of competing cryptocurrencies have emerged, each with its specialties in terms of features, applications, and technologies. Here is a quick primer on alternative currencies:

Key Characteristics of Altcoins:

1. Diverse Features: Alternative cryptocurrencies strive to go above and beyond what Bitcoin offers in terms of

features, enhancements, and innovations. Others place a higher priority on privacy, security, the use of smart contracts, and decentralized applications, while some concentrate on improving transaction speed.

2. Independent Blockchains: A large number of altcoins run on independent blockchains of their own, which means they have unique networks and infrastructure. Tokens, in contrast, are created on established blockchain platforms like Ethereum.

3. Use Cases: Alternative cryptocurrencies (altcoins) have a variety of uses, including enabling decentralized finance (DeFi) applications, enhancing online privacy, and offering fresh consensus mechanisms (like proof of stake).

4. Market Capitalization: The market for cryptocurrencies is dominated by altcoins as a whole. Even though Bitcoin continues to have the largest market capitalization, other cryptocurrencies like Ethereum,

Ripple (XRP), and Litecoin have made significant inroads.

5. Trading Pairs: On different cryptocurrency exchanges, altcoins can be traded against bitcoin, other cryptocurrencies, or fiat money. These trading pairs give traders and investors the chance to diversify their holdings and make price prediction bets.

6. Competition and Innovation: Competition and innovation have been sparked by the existence of altcoins in the cryptocurrency industry. A dynamic ecosystem of digital assets has been developed as a result of the encouragement of the creation of new technologies, consensus mechanisms, and applications.

Common Categories of Altcoins:

1. Privacy Coins: By utilizing cutting-edge encryption techniques, privacy coins like Monero (XMR) and Zcash (ZEC) prioritize user anonymity and privacy.

2. Decentralised application (DApp) and smart contract execution platforms are provided by altcoins like Ethereum (ETH), Binance Coin (BNB), and Cardano (ADA).

3. Forked Coins: A few alternative cryptocurrencies, such as Bitcoin Cash (BCH) and Bitcoin SV (BSV), are forks of the original Bitcoin blockchain that were made to address particular problems or implement protocol changes.

4. Stablecoins: By linking the value of stablecoins to the value of conventional fiat currencies, such as Tether (USDT) and USD Coin (USDC), trading and transfer activities are made easier and more stable.

5. DeFi Tokens: Decentralised finance (DeFi) ecosystems use altcoins like Chainlink (LINK) and Compound (COMP) to facilitate the lending, borrowing, and trading of digital assets.

6. Utility Tokens: In their respective ecosystems, utility tokens like Binance Coin (BNB) and Ethereum Gas (GAS) give users access to particular services, goods, or platforms.

It's critical to remember that the cryptocurrency market is extremely dynamic and that altcoin status can change quickly. When thinking about investing in alternative currencies, it's important to do your homework, comprehend the technology and use cases of each project, and assess the team and community that are supporting it. Furthermore, bear in mind that altcoins can be very volatile, so be ready for big price swings.

7:2 Prominent Altcoins and Their Use Cases

Prominent altcoins have gained recognition and adoption in the cryptocurrency market, each offering unique features and use cases. Here are some notable altcoins and their primary use cases:

1. Ethereum (ETH): Use Case: Decentralised Applications (DApps) and Smart Contracts

- Ethereum is a blockchain platform that enables the development and execution of decentralized applications (DApps) and smart contracts. It serves as a top platform for creating DeFi, NFTs, and other blockchain-based programs.

2. XRP (Ripple):

- Cross-Border Payments Use Case

- Ripple is made to make international payments and remittances more effective and affordable. It aims to offer a quicker and more affordable replacement for conventional banking systems.

3. Litecoin (LTC):

Use Case: Electronic Cash

Litecoin is a peer-to-peer digital currency that is often referred to as "digital silver" and is intended to be used for regular transactions. Compared to Bitcoin, it offers faster confirmation times.

4. Cardano (ADA): Use Case: Scalability and Smart Contracts A blockchain platform called Cardano is well known for emphasizing sustainability, scalability, and academic research. It aims to offer a safe and expandable infrastructure for DApps and smart contracts.

5. LINK: Chainlink

Oracle Services as an Example

- Chainlink is a network of decentralized oracles that links smart contracts to external APIs and real-world data. It is essential to DeFi applications because it offers accurate and dependable data.

6. DOT Polkadot:

- Use Case: Cross-Chain Communication and Interoperability

A more interconnected and effective blockchain ecosystem is fostered by Polkadot, a multi-chain network that allows various blockchains to collaborate and share information.

7. Stellar (XLM): - Use Case: Cross-Border Payments and Financial Inclusion - Stellar aims to promote financial inclusion and facilitate cross-border payments by making it simpler for people and organizations to send money across borders safely and affordably.

8. Monero (XMR)

   - Use Case: Anonymity and Privacy

   - Monero is a cryptocurrency that focuses on privacy and uses cutting-edge cryptography to give users greater anonymity. It is made to provide anonymous and discreet transactions.

9. Tezos (XTZ)

   Smart Contracts and Governance Use Case

   - Tezos is renowned for putting a strong emphasis on on-chain governance, allowing token holders to take part in decision-making regarding network upgrades and improvements. Moreover, smart contracts are supported.

10. Chainlink (LINK): Decentralised Finance (DeFi) Use Case. Compound is a DeFi protocol that enables users to

borrow assets by pledging cryptocurrency as collateral and earning interest on deposited cryptocurrencies. It plays a significant role in the DeFi ecosystem.

11. Uniswap (UNI)

Decentralized Exchange (DEX) Use Case

Uniswap is a decentralized exchange that enables users to swap different cryptocurrencies without the use of a centralized middleman. It is important in the DeFi industry.

12. Aave (AAVE)

Decentralized Lending and Borrowing Use Case

With variable and stable interest rates, the DeFi protocol Aave enables users to lend and borrow cryptocurrencies in a decentralized, non-custodial manner.

These are just a few examples of well-known alternative coins; each has its special features and use cases. When thinking about using or investing in altcoins, it's important to conduct extensive research on each project, evaluate its technology, team, and community support, and comprehend its unique use case within the larger cryptocurrency ecosystem. Be aware that prices can fluctuate widely on the cryptocurrency market, which can be very volatile.

7:3 Token Economy and Initial Coin Offerings (ICOs)

The ecosystem of tokens developed on a blockchain platform is referred to as the "token economy". These tokens are essential to many blockchain applications and services and can represent a wide variety of digital and physical assets. The production, distribution, and use of tokens within a specific blockchain network define token economies. Indicators of token economies include the following:

1. Token Creation: A variety of standards and protocols are used to create tokens on blockchain platforms. For instance, Ethereum-based tokens frequently follow the

ERC-20 standard, which outlines the fundamental guidelines for creating and interacting with tokens. Tokens can stand in for a variety of assets, including virtual money, digital collectibles, membership rights, and more.

2. Token Utility: In a token economy, tokens serve a particular purpose within the connected blockchain network. They can be used in decentralized applications (DApps) to access services, take part in governance, or carry out particular tasks. The regulations and smart contracts governing a token's use determine its utility.

3. Token Distribution: Tokens are given out using several different methods, such as token sales, airdrops, staking, mining, and more. The distribution procedure frequently aims to bring token holders' interests into line with the objectives of the blockchain network.

4. Decentralised Finance (DeFi): Applications for DeFi now frequently use token economies. Tokens are used by DeFi platforms for activities like lending, borrowing,

yield farming, and liquidity provision. These decentralized financial services are made possible by token economies, which are essential.

5. Initial Coin Offerings (ICOs)

- Initial Coin Offerings (ICOs) are a method of raising money by selling a portion of a project's native tokens to investors. To start token economies, ICOs have been a common method.

- ICOs involve the exchange of tokens for cryptocurrencies with investors.

6. Regulation: Different jurisdictions have different rules governing token economies and ICOs. While other nations have adopted more cautious policies or enacted bans, some have implemented clear regulations for ICOs and the use of tokens.

7. Challenges: Token economies face difficulties with scalability, interoperability, and regulatory compliance, to name a few. To ensure sustainability and user

adoption, token economies need to address these problems as they expand.

It's crucial to understand that token economies go beyond ICOs and crowdfunding. They serve as the building blocks of different blockchain ecosystems, allowing decentralized platforms, services, and applications to run. Participants in the token economy must comprehend the value and function of tokens within a particular blockchain network. Additionally, when dealing with tokens and ICOs, regulatory compliance is essential to avoid legal and financial risks.

Chapter 8 Bitcoin's Impact on Society

Since its launch in 2009, Bitcoin has had a significant impact on society in several ways. Some notable effects of Bitcoin on society are listed below:

First, financial inclusion

- Bitcoin has the potential to offer underbanked or unbanked individuals financial services. To store, send, and receive money, people in areas with little access to conventional banking can use Bitcoin.

2. Transfers:

- Bitcoin provides a cheap and effective way to send money across international borders. This can help migrant workers and immigrants who frequently pay exorbitant fees to send money home.

3. Decentralisation and Trust: Since Bitcoin runs on a decentralized, trustless network, ownership and transaction dependencies on a centralized authority are

eliminated. The impact of this characteristic on financial system trust is significant.

4. Indicator of Value:

  - Because of its potential as a store of value, bitcoin is sometimes referred to as "digital gold." Investors looking for protection against inflation and financial instability have been drawn to it.

5. Emerging Financial Services: Bitcoin has spawned a new ecosystem of financial services, including yield farming, lending and borrowing services, and decentralized finance (DeFi) platforms. These platforms are designed to challenge established financial intermediaries.

6. Technology based on blockchain:

  - Blockchain, the technology that powers Bitcoin, has uses outside of cryptocurrencies. Supply chain management, voting procedures, and other areas make use of it.

7. Security and privacy: - Discussions about digital privacy and security have been sparked by Bitcoin. It has emphasized the value of secure storage procedures and private key administration.

8. Debates about currency and monetary policy:

- Bitcoin has sparked discussions about central banking, monetary policy, and the future of money. Some consider it a substitute for conventional currencies and a threat to central banks.

9. Knowledge and Awareness

- The popularity of Bitcoin has raised awareness of blockchain technology and virtual currencies. These ideas are now being introduced to a large number of people who were previously unaware of them.

10. Speculation and Volatility: Speculative traders and investors have been drawn to Bitcoin because of its price volatility and the potential for high returns. Periods of significant price fluctuation have resulted from this.

11. Developments in Law and Regulation:

Governments and regulators from all over the world have been working to create legal frameworks for cryptocurrencies like Bitcoin. This covers tax laws, AML/KYC standards, and licensing requirements for cryptocurrency businesses.

12. New Business Models

- New business models, including cryptocurrency exchanges, wallet providers, mining operations, and payment processors, have been made possible by Bitcoin.

13. Philanthropy and Social Impact: Bitcoin has been used for fundraising and charitable donations, offering an alternative method of aiding social causes.

It's significant to note that there is ongoing discussion about how Bitcoin will affect society. While it has ushered in advantageous changes and new opportunities, it has also drawn criticism and faced difficulties, including potential use in illegal activities and environmental issues related to mining. As the cryptocurrency ecosystem develops and changes to accommodate new developments in technology and circumstances, the function of Bitcoin in society will continue to change.

8:1 Financial Inclusion and Banking the Unbanked

Financial inclusion and the idea of "banking the unbanked" refer to initiatives to give communities and individuals who have historically been shut out of the traditional banking system access to financial services and products. By removing some of the major obstacles that have prevented many people from accessing financial services, bitcoin, and blockchain technology have the potential to significantly contribute to the goal of financial inclusion. The following are some ways that blockchain technology and Bitcoin can promote financial inclusion:

1. Lessened Geographic Barriers: Blockchain technology and Bitcoin operate on a decentralized, global network. As long as they have internet connectivity, people in isolated or underserved areas can access financial services. It does not require a physical bank.

2. Lower Transaction Costs: Cross-border payments, in particular, are frequently subject to high fees when using traditional banking services. Bitcoin makes sending and receiving money more accessible by enabling low-cost, peer-to-peer transactions.

3. Accessibility through Mobile Phones: Despite not having access to traditional banking infrastructure, many people around the world have access to mobile phones. Mobile devices can access and use bitcoin and blockchain-based wallets, enabling financial transactions and services.

4. Security and Ownership: Individuals can directly control and own their Bitcoin and other digital assets with the right knowledge and security precautions. As a

result, there is a lower chance of loss from fraud or bank failure.

5. Savings and Wealth Preservation: In areas where national currencies are unstable or depreciating, bitcoin can act as a store of value and a hedge against inflation. People's wealth and savings may be preserved as a result of this.

6. Financial Services for Microenterprises: By making small-scale microtransactions possible with the help of blockchain technology and bitcoin, microenterprises can now access financial services that were previously unaffordable for traditional banks to offer.

7. Cross-Border Remittances: Bitcoin enables people to send and receive remittances from family members working abroad more quickly and affordably. This is especially important for areas whose economies rely heavily on remittances.

8. Credit Access: Blockchain technology has made it possible to create decentralized lending platforms in the DeFi space that can grant credit to people and businesses without the involvement of a traditional bank.

9. Identity and Documentation: Access to a variety of financial services requires that people be able to establish and verify their identities. Blockchain technology can assist with this. Solutions for decentralized identities can give users more control over their data.

10. Financial Education and Inclusion Initiatives: Groups and initiatives are working to educate and train underserved communities on using Bitcoin and blockchain technology. People are better equipped to navigate the financial digital landscape thanks to these initiatives.

The potential for Bitcoin and blockchain to improve financial inclusion must be kept in mind, but there are also obstacles to be overcome, such as regulatory restrictions, the need for technological literacy, and bridging the digital divide in internet access. To fully reap the rewards of blockchain technology and financial inclusion, cooperation between governments, nonprofits, and the private sector is crucial.

8:2 Bitcoin in Economic Crises

During times of financial instability and economic downturns, Bitcoin has become a hot topic of interest. From different angles, it may play a role in such crises, and its effects may change depending on the particulars of each crisis. Here are a few ways that Bitcoin has been brought up about financial crises:

1. haven and store of value:

   - Bitcoin's potential as a store of value has led to the moniker "digital gold" being applied to it. Some people and investors have turned to Bitcoin as a haven asset during economic crises characterized by currency devaluation, hyperinflation, or financial instability. They see it as a way to shield their wealth from fiat currencies' declining value.

2. Hedging Against Inflation: Bitcoin can act as a hedge against these economic difficulties in areas with high inflation or currency depreciation. Some investors see Bitcoin as a way to maintain their wealth's purchasing power.

3. Accessibility Throughout Financial Crises:
Bitcoin's decentralized nature enables people to access their assets and conduct financial transactions without relying on traditional banks in circumstances where traditional banking systems are stressed or momentarily disrupted.

4. Transactions Across Borders: Sending and receiving money across borders may become difficult during financial crises. Bitcoin provides a substitute for cross-border trade, allowing users to send money to loved ones or carry out international business.

5. Transfers:

- Bitcoin has been used as a more affordable and effective way to receive money from family members working in other countries in regions that depend on remittances from abroad.

6. Financial Inclusion

- By enabling people to participate in the global economy through digital wallets and transactions, Bitcoin can offer a means of financial inclusion in places with limited access to traditional financial services.

7. Speculative Investment: Due to the uncertainty that economic crises can cause, some people may opt to make speculative investments. During these times, speculative traders and investors have been attracted to Bitcoin due to its potential for price appreciation.

8. Greater Adoption and Knowledge

- Economic crises frequently result in a rise in Bitcoin and cryptocurrency awareness. In times of financial instability, people who may not have previously thought about or understood digital assets may start to show an interest in them.

While Bitcoin has occasionally demonstrated its potential as a hedge and haven asset, it is important to remember that it also carries some inherent risks. Because of its notorious price volatility, bitcoin's value can change dramatically. In addition, local regulatory and legal considerations may differ and have an impact on how and where Bitcoin is used and adopted during economic downturns.

Research and discussion on the subject of Bitcoin's role in economic crises are ongoing. Its effects can vary greatly depending on the type of crisis, the state of the local economy, and the level of adoption of digital assets in the area. People and investors thinking about incorporating Bitcoin into their financial plan during crises should do so with a

8:3 Social and Political Implication

Bitcoin has significant social and political ramifications that could have a variety of effects on society. Here are some important things to keep in mind:

Social Consequences:

1. Financial Inclusion: Especially in areas with limited access to traditional banking infrastructure, Bitcoin has the potential to advance financial inclusion by giving underbanked or unbanked individuals access to financial services.

2. Economic Empowerment: By using Bitcoin, people can have more control over their financial resources. It enables asset transfers without the use of middlemen, enabling users to manage their wealth more directly.

3. Digital Privacy: People who are concerned about their privacy in the digital world may find solace in Bitcoin's potential to provide enhanced financial privacy and control over their financial data.

4. Education and Awareness: The emergence of Bitcoin has stoked interest in blockchain and financial technology. To raise public awareness of cryptocurrencies and the potential they offer, educational initiatives and awareness campaigns have been launched.

5. Community and Advocacy: Bitcoin has helped to create a global community of supporters, developers, and advocates who are interested in decentralized financial systems, digital currencies, and other related topics.

Political Consequences:

1. Monetary Policy and Central Banks: Bitcoin questions central banks' traditional functions and their authority over monetary policy. It makes one wonder what role central banking will play in a world where digital currencies are decentralized.

2. Compliance and Regulation: Governments and regulatory organizations are working to create guidelines and rules for Bitcoin and other cryptocurrencies. There are disagreements over the best ways to regulate digital

assets because the regulatory environment differs from one nation to the next.

3. Privacy and Surveillance: Privacy and surveillance are impacted by the use of Bitcoin in financial transactions. While supporters stress the value of financial privacy, some governments are concerned about its potential to facilitate illegal activities.

4. International Relations: Due to its global nature, bitcoin may have an impact on trade, financial systems, and international relations. It has sparked discussions at international forums and has the potential to affect cross-border transactions.

5. Technological Innovation: The creation of blockchain technology and new methods for designing digital payment systems were both sparked by Bitcoin. Beyond cryptocurrencies, governments and institutions are looking into the potential uses of blockchain technology.

6. Decentralisation and Trust: The decentralized nature of Bitcoin calls into question long-held beliefs about how much one can trust centralized financial systems. The implications for the ideas of trust and governance may be more extensive as a result.

7. Digital Rights and Ownership: Concerns about digital rights and intellectual property are raised by the possession and management of digital assets. As blockchain technology spreads, the idea of digital ownership is changing.

It's crucial to remember that there are still ongoing discussions and debates about the social and political implications of Bitcoin. Regulatory decisions, technological developments, and public perceptions are just a few of the variables that influence how technology affects society. As Bitcoin expands in popularity and adoption, its place in the broader financial and political landscape continues to change.

Chapter 9 Challenges and Controversies

Like any disruptive technology, bitcoin has experienced several difficulties and controversies over the years. These issues have influenced ongoing discussions and debates among policymakers and in the cryptocurrency community. Here are some of the significant issues and debates surrounding Bitcoin:

1. Regulatory Uncertainty

Regulatory obstacles have been a recurring problem for Bitcoin. A complex and frequently ambiguous legal environment has resulted from the different approaches that different nations have taken to regulate cryptocurrencies.

2. Criminal Use: Due to its pseudonymous nature, Bitcoin has raised questions about its potential use in nefarious activities like money laundering, tax evasion, and shady online deals.

3. Volatility

- The price volatility of Bitcoin has been a significant issue. Some investors see it as a potential asset that will increase in value, but others find it difficult to use as a reliable store of value or medium of exchange.

4. Scalability

- Bitcoin's network has trouble scaling due to its low transaction throughput. As a result, there has been congestion during times of high demand and an increase in transaction fees.

5 Energy Consumption: The environmental impact of Bitcoin mining has been questioned due to the energy requirements, particularly for proof-of-work blockchains. Critics contend that it causes climate change and carbon emissions.

6. Technological advancements

- It can be hard for the Bitcoin community to come to a consensus on technological advancements and improvements. This sparked discussions and even forks, like the splits of Bitcoin Cash and Bitcoin SV.

7. Security Threats

  - Risks relating to the security of wallets, hacks of exchanges, and potential weaknesses in the Bitcoin network or its underlying technology are among the security concerns.

8. Initial Coin Offerings, or ICOs, include: Although unrelated to Bitcoin, concerns about fraudulent and unregulated fundraising in the cryptocurrency space were raised by the ICO boom and subsequent crash.

9. Reporting and Taxation:

  - There has been debate over how to report cryptocurrency holdings for tax purposes. Tax authorities have worked to make sure that cryptocurrency users accurately report their income.

10. Conflicts in Law and Regulation:

  - Legal issues involving fraud, security lapses, and regulatory compliance have been raised about Bitcoin and blockchain projects. There have been some well-known cases that have led to lawsuits and court agreements.

11. Centralization Concerns:

- Despite being decentralized, worries have been raised about the concentration of mining power in some areas, which may jeopardize the security and integrity of the network.

12. Social and ethical issues:

- Concerns about wealth inequality and the concentration of wealth among early adopters have been linked to Bitcoin as social and ethical issues.

13. Adoption Obstacles

- The widespread acceptance of Bitcoin as a form of payment and a store of value is still difficult to achieve because of issues with usability, technological limitations, and public skepticism.

14. Stablecoins are under regulatory scrutiny: - Because of their reserves, issuance, and potential effects on the

larger financial system, stablecoins like USDC and Tether have come under regulatory scrutiny.

These difficulties and controversies are a natural part of the developing and quickly changing cryptocurrency industry. Technical innovation, regulatory clarity, market participants acting responsibly, and a thorough understanding of the advantages and disadvantages of blockchain technology and digital assets are all necessary to address these issues. As the technology develops, the cryptocurrency community and policymakers are still battling these issues.

9:1 Scalability Issues and Network Upgrades

Since their inception, scaling problems and network upgrades have been one of the main obstacles for Bitcoin and other blockchain networks. A network's ability to handle an increasing volume of transactions and users while maintaining effectiveness and low costs is referred to as scalability. Due to Bitcoin's limited scalability, network upgrades have been the subject of numerous discussions and debates. Here are some crucial details about these difficulties:

scaling problems

1. Block Size Limit: A 1 MB block size limit was incorporated into the original design of Bitcoin, limiting the number of transactions that can be processed in a block. When there is a lot of demand, this limit may become congested, which would mean longer confirmation times and more expensive transactions.

2. Transaction Throughput: The block size and block time (10 minutes) of Bitcoin impose a limit on transaction throughput. Because of this, Bitcoin can only handle a small number of transactions per second, which is too few for a global payment network.

3. Increasing User Base: Scalability issues have gotten worse as a result of Bitcoin's rising popularity. The network's capacity is put under more strain as a result of more users and transactions.

Network improvements:

Several upgrade proposals have been taken into consideration, and in some cases, implemented, to address scalability issues and enhance the Bitcoin network:

1. Segregated Witness (SegWit): SegWit was introduced in 2017 and effectively increased the block size limit without a hard fork by separating witness data from transaction data. More transactions per block were possible thanks to this upgrade.

2. Lightning Network: Running on top of the Bitcoin blockchain, the Lightning Network is a second-layer solution. Off-chain transactions are made possible, greatly enhancing the network's ability to handle microtransactions and lowering costs.

3. Taproot: In late 2021, a network upgrade called Taproot was put into effect. It includes some scalability improvements but primarily focuses on privacy and security upgrades.

4. Schnorr Signatures: Although not yet in use, Schnorr signatures are an upgrade that has been suggested. They may help to reduce the amount of transaction data and increase the number of transactions that can fit into a block.

5. Additional Block Size Discussions: Some members of the Bitcoin community are still in favor of raising the block size restriction. This subject is still debatable, though, because there are issues with centralization and security trade-offs related to bigger blocks.

6. Layer-2 Solutions: State chains and sidechains are two additional layer-2 solutions being created and implemented to improve Bitcoin's scalability, in addition to the Lightning Network.

It's crucial to remember that any network upgrade within the Bitcoin ecosystem requires agreement from miners, developers, node operators, and the general public. Consensus on significant protocol changes can be difficult to reach and frequently necessitates protracted discussions and debates.

The Bitcoin community is still working to solve the scalability and network upgrade problems. While maintaining the network's decentralization, security, and trustlessness, solutions aim to increase its capacity. It is anticipated that additional innovations and upgrades will continue to address these issues as Bitcoin develops.

9:2 Privacy and Security Concerns

In the world of Bitcoin and cryptocurrencies, privacy and security concerns are crucial factors. Even though Bitcoin provides some financial privacy, it is not completely anonymous, and security issues can occur throughout the Bitcoin ecosystem. The following are some of the main privacy and security issues with bitcoin:

Privacy issues:

1. Pseudonymity: Transactions made using Bitcoin are pseudonymous, which means they are not directly associated with users' real-world identities. The blockchain, a public ledger, keeps track of all Bitcoin transactions, making them potentially traceable.

2. Reusing Bitcoin addresses can compromise privacy, according to number two. It is simpler to connect several transactions to a single user or entity when they are linked to the same address.

3. Blockchain Analysis: Advanced strategies and methods, like blockchain analysis, can be used to de-anonymize Bitcoin users. Users who value their privacy are concerned about this.

4. Linkability: When transactions have similar transaction patterns or share input addresses, they can be linked together and may reveal information about users.

5. Exchange and KYC/AML: Users' identities can be linked to their transactions when they buy Bitcoin on

exchanges that demand Know Your Customer (KYC) and Anti-Money Laundering (AML) compliance.

6. Chain Analysis Companies: Several businesses focus on conducting forensic, compliance, and investigative blockchain analyses, which may compromise user privacy.

Security Concerns:

1. Custodial Risks: Because exchanges and custodial wallets are prone to hacking and security breaches, storing Bitcoin in either of these places entails security risks. Users must have faith in third parties with their money and private keys.

2. Phishing and Scams: To trick users into disclosing private keys or sending Bitcoin to phony addresses, malicious actors frequently use phishing websites, social engineering, and fraudulent schemes.

3. Malware and keyloggers: Unwanted access to cryptocurrency wallets can be obtained by malicious

software, which can also steal private keys from users' devices and compromise device security.

4. Centralization of Mining Power: The security and decentralization of the network may be at risk if mining power is concentrated in the hands of a small number of entities.

5. Software Vulnerabilities: Bitcoin clients and wallets may be susceptible to security flaws. To reduce risks, regular updates and best practices are required.

6. Physical Threats: Users are responsible for preventing loss, theft, and damage to their physical wallet devices and recovery seeds. The loss of money could result from failure to do so.

7. Double Spending: Although Bitcoin's consensus mechanism is intended to prevent double spending, attacks that try to spend the same Bitcoin twice can occur in some circumstances, especially with shorter confirmation times.

8. Regulatory and Legal Risks: Legal actions against users and service providers as well as regulatory changes may have an impact.

Users of Bitcoin can take several actions to allay these worries and improve privacy and security:
Use non-custodial wallets to store your Bitcoin to reduce the risk of third-party custody. In non-custodial wallets, users maintain control over their private keys.
- Implement Best Practices: Updating software frequently, using strong, unique passwords, and enabling two-factor authentication are all examples of best security practices that can enhance security.
- Discover Privacy Tools: To increase the anonymity of their transactions, privacy-conscious users can investigate tools like CoinJoin, CoinSwap, and privacy-focused wallets.
- Educate Themselves: To avoid scams and phishing attempts, users should educate themselves about the risks and use critical thinking.

- Make Use Of Secure Hardware Wallets: By storing private keys offline, hardware wallets offer a high level of protection against online threats.

In the Bitcoin ecosystem, addressing privacy and security issues is a continuous process. To guarantee a secure and private experience for Bitcoin users, a combination of technological advancements, user education, and responsible practice is needed.

9:3 Ethical and Environmental Debates

The following principal issues dominate discussions on Bitcoin's ethics and environment:

1. Energy Use and the Effect on the Environment
   - Concerns about Bitcoin's environmental impact have been raised due to its high energy consumption, particularly during the mining process. The proof-of-work (PoW) consensus mechanism used in Bitcoin mining consumes a lot of processing power. According to critics, this energy use increases carbone

missions and causes climate change. Supporters contend that the potential advantages of a decentralized financial system should be weighed against the environmental impact.

2. Hardware and E-Waste Disposal: - The mining industry is experiencing a rapid evolution of hardware, making older, less effective equipment obsolete. Environmental issues arise when electronic waste (or "e-waste") is disposed of. Although some Bitcoin miners have made an effort to recycle or repurpose old hardware, this issue still exists.

3. The concentration of mining power

- Environmental sustainability issues may arise as a result of the concentration of mining power and the fact that a sizable portion of mining occurs in areas with affordable electricity. Coal-based energy, which can be particularly carbon-intensive, may be heavily used in some areas.

4. Financial Inclusion and Ethics: Bitcoin has the potential to help people in areas with limited access to traditional banking become financially included and empowered. According to supporters, this promotes social and economic equity. However, there are worries that early adopters and wealthy people may benefit from Bitcoin disproportionately, potentially escalating wealth inequality.

5. Ethics and digital privacy:

  - Although Bitcoin has some advantages in terms of privacy, it is not entirely anonymous. The use of Bitcoin for illegal activities has sparked ethical questions, and some governments have taken action to stop illicit cryptocurrency activity.

6. Investing ethically: - Different people and organizations have different views on the ethical ramifications of investing in Bitcoin. Some investors and funds have decided to invest some of their funds in Bitcoin and other cryptocurrencies because they see them as a potential inflation hedge and store of value.

Others worry about the moral ramifications of taking part in a financial system that is decentralized from traditional banking and governed by law.

7. Regulatory and Legal Challenges:

- There are significant regional differences in the legal and regulatory environment for bitcoin. While other governments and regulators have adopted a more cautious or restrictive approach, some have adopted regulations to address issues like know-your-customer (KYC) requirements and anti-money laundering (AML).

Addressing these ethical and environmental issues is a difficult task that calls for taking into account several variables, such as the technology's potential advantages and disadvantages, technological innovations, governmental policies, and societal values. The development of sustainable mining techniques and efforts to make Bitcoin more energy-efficient through alternative consensus mechanisms like proof of stake (PoS) may help allay some of these worries. Additionally, as people become more aware of these problems, there may be more discussions and initiatives to find solutions that adhere to moral and ethical standards.

Chapter 10 The Future of Bitcoin

Since Bitcoin has the potential to keep changing the financial landscape and evolving in many different ways, its future is a subject of intense interest and speculative discussion. Though we cannot predict the future with absolute certainty, we can pinpoint several crucial factors that will probably influence how Bitcoin develops in the future:

1. Adoption and Integration:

   - The adoption and integration of Bitcoin into the global financial system will have a significant impact on its future. Bitcoin may become a more commonplace method of payment and a store of value as more companies, organizations, and people accept and use it.

2. Regulatory Frameworks: Bitcoin's future will be significantly shaped by the regulatory landscape for cryptocurrencies. To address issues with taxation, anti-money laundering, consumer protection, and other issues, governments and regulatory bodies are working

to establish legal frameworks and policies for digital assets.

3. Technological Progress

- The utility and security of Bitcoin will continue to be improved by ongoing technological developments, such as the adoption of scaling solutions, enhanced privacy features, and improvements in wallet security.

Scalability and Layer-2 Approaches: The Lightning Network and other layer-2 protocols are scaling solutions that try to solve the scalability problems with Bitcoin. They have the potential to significantly improve the network's ability to handle transactions.

5. Participation by Institutions:

- Institutional investors and financial institutions are anticipated to become more active in the bitcoin market. Increased liquidity, stability, and acceptance of Bitcoin as an asset class may result from institutional adoption.

6. Financialization: The incorporation of Bitcoin into established financial systems, including the creation of Bitcoin exchange-traded funds (ETFs) and other financial instruments, may strengthen Bitcoin's standing as an investment.

7. Transactions Across Borders:

- Particularly in areas with limited access to international banking services, Bitcoin's potential as a cross-border payment solution may continue to develop.

8. Privacy and Security Improvements: - User privacy is expected to be improved by privacy enhancements like confidential transactions, Schnorr signatures, and Taproot. To counter threats and vulnerabilities, security measures will keep developing.

9. Geopolitical factors include:

- Bitcoin's role in global politics and economics may continue to change, especially in areas that are experiencing financial crises, devaluation of their currencies, and economic instability.

10. Technological rivalry:

   - Blockchain projects and other cryptocurrencies will continue to compete with Bitcoin. The role and development of Bitcoin may be influenced by the development of the larger crypto ecosystem.

11. Public Perception and Awareness: - As more people learn about and become aware of Bitcoin, it may come to be seen as a more reliable medium of exchange and a digital store of value.

12. Environmental and ethical issues:

   - Bitcoin-related ethical and environmental discussions may influence changes in the cryptocurrency ecosystem, such as a move to more sustainable consensus mechanisms or a rise in the use of environmentally friendly mining techniques.

13. New developments and use cases:

   - The emergence of novel use cases, such as smart contracts, non-fungible tokens (NFTs), and decentralized finance (DeFi), could increase the usefulness of Bitcoin beyond its existing applications.

It's important to remember that Bitcoin has problems and unknowns, just like any other technology or financial asset. Its future will be influenced by a complex interaction of societal trends, market dynamics, regulatory decisions, and technological advancements. Even though Bitcoin has come a long way since its inception, its journey is far from over, and people, organizations, and the international financial community will be closely watching its development.

10:1 Scaling Solutions: Lightning Network and Segregated Witness

Two significant scaling solutions that have been integrated into the Bitcoin network to address its scalability issues are the Lightning Network and Segregated Witness (SegWit). Here is a description of each:

Witness Segregated (SegWit):

In August 2017, Segregated Witness, a significant Bitcoin network upgrade, went live. Its main goal was to increase Bitcoin's scalability and deal with some transaction malleability issues. These are the main features of SegWit:

1. Transaction Malleability: SegWit reorganizes data storage in Bitcoin blocks by separating witness data (the information required to confirm a transaction's digital signature) from transaction data. This division reduces transaction malleability, which is the ability to change a transaction's ID without having the transaction become invalid. The Lightning Network and other layer-2 solutions become more effective and secure once this problem is resolved.

2. More Block Space SegWit increases the block size limit by eliminating the signature data from the block size calculation. As a result, a block can accommodate more transactions without actually growing in size. This lessens transaction fees and congestion.

3. Backward Compatibility: SegWit keeps older Bitcoin clients backward compatible, allowing users who have not upgraded to continue using the network. However, not all wallets and exchanges support SegWit transactions, so not all transactions take advantage of the lower fees and enhanced security.

4. Multi-Signature Security SegWit introduces enhancements to multi-signature transactions' security. It improves the script language to provide multi-signature wallets with stronger security.

Thunderbolt Network

On top of the Bitcoin blockchain, there is a second-layer scaling solution called the Lightning Network. It aims to make off-chain transactions quick, affordable, and scalable possible. The Lightning Network's main features are as follows:

1. Off-Chain Transactions: The Lightning Network enables users to build off-chain payment channels. Multiple transactions can be carried out through these

channels without being directly added to the Bitcoin blockchain. This lowers costs and congestion on the main chain.

2. Near-instantaneous Transactions: The Lightning Network is well suited for small, routine payments like coffee or microtransactions because it offers nearly instantaneous transactions. Unlike the 10-minute block confirmation time on the Bitcoin blockchain, these transactions are confirmed instantly.

3. Scalability: The Lightning Network greatly increases Bitcoin's ability to process transactions. With only a small fee and without clogging the main blockchain, users can send and receive payments.

4. Lower Transaction Fees: Compared to conventional on-chain transactions, Lightning Network transactions typically have lower transaction fees because the majority of transactions take place off-chain.

5. Routing Nodes: Users must connect to routing nodes to use the Lightning Network. By distributing payments among users, these nodes streamline transactions. Routing nodes receive modest compensation for their services.

6. Security: Security is a top priority in the Lightning Network's design. To settle their balances on the main blockchain, users can shut down their payment channels whenever they want. This prevents money from becoming frozen.

The scalability of Bitcoin could be greatly enhanced by the Lightning Network, making it a more effective and flexible payment system. However, it is still in its early stages of development and adoption, and some issues need to be resolved for wider adoption, such as routing effectiveness and liquidity management.

In conclusion, Segregated Witness and the Lightning Network are complementary solutions that address various scalability issues with Bitcoin in different ways.

While the Lightning Network provides off-chain scaling and quick, inexpensive transactions, SegWit enhances the security and scalability of on-chain transactions. With the help of these solutions, Bitcoin should become more effective, available, and adaptable for both users and businesses.

10:2 Environmental Concerns and Sustainable Mining

Energy usage related to the proof-of-work (PoW) mining process is the main source of environmental worries regarding Bitcoin. To validate transactions and add new blocks to the blockchain, the PoW consensus mechanism must be solved to secure the Bitcoin network. Although essential for network security, this process uses a lot of computational power and consequently uses a lot of energy. Following are some important environmental issues and initiatives to address them:

Environmental Concerns:

1. Carbon Emissions: Because Bitcoin mining uses a lot of energy, its carbon footprint has drawn attention. In areas with low electricity costs, miners frequently use fossil fuels, particularly coal, which can increase carbon emissions.

2. E-Waste: As mining hardware has evolved quickly, older, less effective equipment has been thrown out, raising issues with electronic waste (e-waste).

3. Depletion of Resources: The mining of bitcoins requires the use of hardware, particularly semiconductors and graphics cards. Resource depletion and supply chain issues may result from this.

Efforts to Address Environmental Concerns:
1. The switch to renewable energy sources is underway for some Bitcoin miners and mining operations. These include hydroelectric, wind, and solar energy, which can lessen the negative effects of mining on the environment.

2. Green Mining Initiatives: To reduce their carbon footprint, some businesses and mining firms are implementing eco-friendly procedures and investing in green technologies.

3. Carbon Offsetting: To reduce their emissions, some mining operations invest in carbon offset projects. These initiatives, like reforestation or renewable energy initiatives, aim to lower emissions in other industries.

4. Energy Efficiency: Work is being done to create mining equipment that uses less energy. The security of the network is maintained while using less energy by newer equipment.

5. Geographical Relocation: To take advantage of cleaner energy options, miners are looking into areas with a lot of renewable energy sources, like Iceland and Scandinavia.

6. Public Awareness and Pressure: Raising public awareness of the environmental risks posed by Bitcoin mining may result in pressure being applied to the sector to adopt more environmentally friendly procedures.

7. Switch to Proof of Stake (PoS): PoS is a different consensus mechanism that doesn't require mining, which uses a lot of energy. PoS is being adopted by some cryptocurrencies, including Ethereum, to lessen their carbon footprint.

8. Efficiency through Layer-2 Solutions: By reducing the number of on-chain transactions, such as the Lightning Network, less energy is needed for validation.

It's crucial to remember that, despite efforts to make Bitcoin mining more environmentally friendly, the switch to cleaner energy sources and hardware that uses less energy is still in progress. Coordination between miners, researchers, governments, and the cryptocurrency community is necessary to address the environmental issues raised by Bitcoin.

It is anticipated that as the industry develops, more importance will be given to environmentally friendly and sustainable practices in Bitcoin mining and the larger blockchain ecosystem.

10:3 The Evolving Role of Bitcoin in the Financial World

Since its launch in 2009, Bitcoin's position in the financial sector has significantly changed. A global asset class and financial infrastructure have evolved from what was once an experimental digital currency. The following are the main changes in Bitcoin's role in the financial sector:

1. Store of Value and digital gold
   - Bitcoin, also known as "digital gold," is becoming more and more recognized as a store of value. Investors see it as a way to protect their wealth from inflation and increase it during uncertain economic times.

2. Investing Instrument:

  - Both institutional and individual investors have accepted Bitcoin as a form of investment. Parts of the portfolios of hedge funds, asset managers, and publicly traded companies are invested in Bitcoin.

3. Asset Diversification: As a means of diversification, Bitcoin has been incorporated into conventional financial portfolios. It provides a non-correlated asset that can help investment portfolios balance risk.

4. A solution for payments and remittances

  - Although not its primary use, Bitcoin is used for cross-border transactions and international remittances, providing a practical and affordable alternative to conventional payment methods.

5. Decentralised Finance

  - Bitcoin is starting to have an impact on the ecosystem of decentralized finance (DeFi). Owners of Bitcoin can participate in DeFi applications and earn yield by using Wrapped Bitcoin (WBTC) and other tokens.

6. Custody and Financial Services: Financial institutions offer secure storage and access to Bitcoin as well as custody and trading services.

7. Adoption in Institutions:

   - Well-known financial companies like Fidelity, PayPal, and Square have incorporated Bitcoin into their platforms and are now providing services for buying, selling, and holding Bitcoin.

8. Market for Derivatives:

   - The Bitcoin futures and options markets have developed, enabling both institutional and retail traders to diversify their exposure and make predictions about the course of the cryptocurrency's price.

9. Regulatory Frameworks: Bitcoin has become more widely accepted due to regulatory clarity and growing acceptance of it as a valid financial asset.

10. Economic Inclusion:

- Bitcoin has the potential to help people who don't have access to traditional banking services become financially included, especially in places with poor infrastructure.

11. Privacy and Financial Sovereignty: Bitcoin appeals to people who value their financial independence by giving users some degree of financial privacy and control over their assets.
Innovations and Ecosystem Development:

With advancements in wallet technology, scalability fixes, and the emergence of layer-2 protocols, the Bitcoin ecosystem has grown and become more diverse.

13. Political and economic uncertainty around the world:

- Bitcoin is viewed as a hedge against such uncertainties in areas dealing with economic instability, currency devaluation, or financial crises.

14. Public Awareness and Education: - Public awareness and adoption of Bitcoin have increased as a result of

increased efforts to inform the public about its potential and risks.

15. Environmental and ethical considerations:
Discussions and increased awareness of sustainable practices in the Bitcoin and larger cryptocurrency industries are the result of ethical and environmental debates.

The changing place of Bitcoin in the financial sector is a reflection of its maturation and expanding legitimacy as an asset class. Although it hasn't supplanted conventional fiat currencies, it has emerged as a significant improvement to the world's financial system. Regulation changes, technological advancements, and institutional and individual adoption will all have an impact on how Bitcoin is used in finance in the future.

Chapter 11 Building a Bitcoin Portfolio

Careful planning, risk management, and adherence to your investment objectives are required when creating a Bitcoin portfolio. The following actions should be taken into account when building a Bitcoin portfolio:

Set definite investment objectives:

- Establish your investment goals. Do you want to make short-term speculative gains, long-term wealth preservation, or something in between? Your portfolio strategy will be influenced by your objectives.

2. Tolerance for Risk:

- Evaluate your risk appetite. Bitcoin's price turbulence is well-known. Recognize the level of risk you are willing and able to accept.

3. Diversification: To spread risk, diversify your Bitcoin holdings. To create a well-balanced investment portfolio, take into account allocating funds to additional assets in addition to Bitcoin, such as stocks, bonds, or real estate.

4. Asset Management:

- Choose how much of your overall investment portfolio you want to put towards Bitcoin. Your allocation should be in line with your investment objectives and risk tolerance.

5. Horizon of the Investment:

- Choose a time frame for your investments. Are you looking to invest for the long run, the medium run, or the short run? Your investment strategy will be influenced by your time horizon.

6. Dollar Cost Averaging (DCA): Using the DCA strategy, you make regular, fixed-amount investments regardless of the price. This strategy can lessen the effects of market turbulence and emotional choices.

7. Safekeeping:

- Select safe options for Bitcoin storage. To safeguard your assets, think about using hardware wallets, paper wallets, or trusted custodial services.

8. Keep Current:

- Stay up to date on the newest developments in Bitcoin and the cryptocurrency industry. Your investment strategy may be impacted by modifications to legislation, market sentiment, and technology.

9. Steer clear of FOMO and panic buying: Don't let feelings influence your choice of investments. Avoid panic selling during market downturns and FOMO during price rallies. Maintain your investment strategy.

10. Risk Administration:

- Use risk management techniques to protect your capital, such as placing stop-loss orders or employing a predetermined exit strategy.

11. Long-Term Viewpoint

- Consider a long-term approach. Although the price of bitcoin can be extremely volatile in the short term, it has significantly increased over time.

12. Watch out for Scams and Fraud: Be wary of phishing scams and fraudulent schemes. Verify the legitimacy of the services you use and only use reputable exchanges and wallets.

Considerations Regarding Taxes:

- Recognise how investing in Bitcoin will affect your taxes. To comply with the law, you must accurately report your gains and losses.

14. Consult a Professional:

Consider speaking with a financial advisor who is knowledgeable about cryptocurrencies if you are unsure of your investment strategy or how to create a Bitcoin portfolio.

Keep in mind that the cryptocurrency market can be unpredictable and highly speculative. Before making an investment decision, it is critical to do extensive research and only invest money that you can afford to lose. Building a Bitcoin portfolio is an individual endeavor, so your plan should reflect your financial objectives and risk appetite.

11:1 Portfolio Diversification Strategies

By spreading risk among various asset classes, diversifying your investment portfolio can help to lower overall risk and possibly improve returns. Long-term investment strategies that emphasize diversification are generally accepted. Following are a few portfolio diversification techniques:

1. Diversification of Asset Classes:

   - Diversify your portfolio by including various asset classes, such as stocks, bonds, real estate, and alternative investments (like cryptocurrencies like Bitcoin). Risk-return profiles for various asset classes vary.

2. Geographic Diversification: - Purchase assets from various regions of the world. Your portfolio can be protected from country-specific political or economic risks by utilizing international diversification.

3. Diversification of Industry:

- Diversify your portfolio across various sectors and industries when it comes to equity investments. This strategy can aid in reducing the risks connected to sector-specific events.

4. Diversification of Market Cap:
  - When making equity investments, think about diversifying among stocks in the large--, mid-, and small-cap categories of market capitalization. Every one of them has unique risk-return characteristics.

5. Investment Style Diversification: - Spread your money among various investment philosophies, such as value, growth, or a mix of both. Every style performs differently depending on the market environment.

6. Diversification of Bonds:
  - In fixed income, diversify your bond holdings by investing in a range of bonds, such as high-yield, municipal, corporate, and government issues. Bonds come in a variety of yields and credit risk levels.

7. Diversification of the Time Horizon:

- When diversifying, take your investment time horizon into account. Short-term investments might necessitate a more cautious approach, whereas longer-term investments might permit greater risk-taking.

8. Cash and Liquidity: - Keep enough cash on hand or in cash equivalents to cover unexpected expenses and seize investment opportunities. Flexibility can be derived from your portfolio's liquidity.

9. Diverse Investments

- To further diversify and possibly lower risk, think about including alternative investments, such as real estate, commodities, and cryptocurrencies, in your portfolio.

10. Readjusting:

- Rebalance your portfolio regularly to keep it at the desired asset allocation. Your portfolio may stray from its initial allocation over time as asset values change.

11. Tolerance for Risk:

- Match your risk tolerance to the diversification of your portfolio. More aggressive diversification may be possible if one has a higher risk tolerance.

12. Professional Guidance:

- If you're unsure about portfolio diversification, speak with a financial advisor who can help you create an investment strategy that is diversified and suited to your risk tolerance and financial objectives.

The effect of market volatility and economic events on your investment portfolio can be lessened with diversification. It's crucial to realize that diversification does not eliminate investment risk, but it can help spread risk across various assets, potentially resulting in a more comfortable investing experience over time.

11:2 Long-Term vs. Short-Term Investing

The management of investments can be done in two different ways: long-term investing and short-term investing. Each has its advantages, disadvantages, and considerations. A comparison of long-term and short-term investing is provided below:

Investing for the future:

1. Time Horizon: Long-term investing typically entails holding investments for a considerable amount of time, which is frequently expressed in years or even decades.

2. Investment Objectives: Long-term investors frequently seek to accomplish monetary objectives like retirement planning, financing education, or gradually accumulating wealth.

3. Risk Tolerance: Because they have a longer time horizon to withstand market fluctuations, long-term investors can typically afford to take on more risk in their portfolio.

4. Asset Selection: Common long-term investments include diversified mutual funds or exchange-traded funds (ETFs), stocks, bonds, and real estate. Over time, these assets usually increase in value.

5. Diversification: To lower risk, long-term investors frequently emphasize diversification. They aim for steady, consistent growth and hold a variety of assets to spread risk.

6. Buy and Hold: Long-term investors frequently use a buy-and-hold strategy. They invest in assets they think will increase in value and hold onto them through market fluctuations.

7. Tax Considerations: Generally speaking, long-term capital gains are taxed at a lower rate than short-term gains. Gaining tax benefits requires holding investments for at least a year.

8. Less Trading: Long-term investors engage in less trading, which lowers transaction fees and potential capital gains taxes.

Short-Term Investing:

1. Time Horizon: Short-term investing refers to the practice of holding investments for a short amount of time, which can be anything from a few minutes (day trading) to a few years.

2. Investment Objectives: Short-term investors frequently seek to profit from price changes or market events to make quick gains. They might not give much thought to long-term financial objectives.

3. Risk Tolerance: Due to their potential sensitivity to market volatility and potential losses, short-term investors typically have a lower risk tolerance.

4. Asset Selection Stocks, options, cryptocurrencies, and commodities are typical short-term investments. These

assets are frequently chosen because of the possibility of swift price changes.

5. Speculation: Short-term investors frequently engage in speculative trading to make money off of changes in the market or particular events.

6. Active Trading: To take advantage of swift price changes, short-term investors frequently engage in active trading, buying and selling assets more frequently.

7. Tax Considerations: There may be taxes associated with each trade, and short-term capital gains are frequently subject to higher tax rates. The overall return on investment may be impacted by this.

8. Emotion-driven: Decisions made by short-term investors may be more influenced by news events and market sentiment than by long-term investors.

Your financial objectives, level of risk tolerance, and investment strategies will determine whether you choose to invest long-term or short-term. Understanding your goals and the amount of time you can devote to managing your investments is crucial. To balance potential gains and risk, many investors decide to mix long-term and short-term investments. Whatever your chosen time horizon, diversification is a crucial factor in creating a well-rounded investment portfolio.

11:3 Staying Informed and Making Informed Decisions

Making informed decisions and maintaining knowledge is crucial for successful investing. Here are some tips to keep you informed and assist you in making wise investment decisions:

1. Ongoing Education:
   - Maintain up-to-date knowledge of current events and market trends. Read investing-related books, articles, research reports, and go to investing-related seminars or webinars.

2. Variety of Information Sources

- Gather information from a range of sources, such as reputable financial publications, financial news websites, analyst reports, and official reports from governmental organizations.

Follow these key indicators: 3. Pay attention to important economic indicators like interest rates, inflation, and GDP growth. These indicators can inform investment choices and offer information about the state of the economy as a whole.

4. Recognise Financial Instruments:

- Know a financial product's workings, risk profile, and potential returns before investing. This entails reading the terms and conditions of other investments as well as the prospectus for investment funds.

5. Risk Assessment: Evaluate your financial objectives and risk tolerance. Recognize that various investments carry varying degrees of risk, and select investments that fit your risk tolerance.

6. Ensure Portfolio Diversity:

- Diversification can aid in risk reduction. To spread risk and potential losses, distribute your investments across a variety of asset classes and geographical areas.

7. Investment Plan:

- Create a detailed investment plan. Choose between long-term investing and short-term trading as your investment strategy. Make a plan and follow it.

8. Professional Advice: Seek the advice of a financial advisor or investment professional to help you make decisions, particularly if you are unfamiliar with investing or working with complex financial products.

9. Remain Cool and Avoid Emotionally Driven Decisions:

- Impulsive actions brought on by emotional decisions may not be in your best interests. Maintain your investment strategy despite market turbulence.

10. Continual portfolio evaluation:

- Regularly check to see if your investment portfolio is still in line with your financial objectives. Based on modifications to your life, goals, or market circumstances, make adjustments as necessary.

11. Risk Management: Protect your investments from sizable losses by using risk management strategies, such as placing stop-loss orders.

12. Maintain Records:

- Keep thorough records of your investments, including the dates, costs, and justifications for your choices. This aids in tax reporting and helps you learn from your mistakes.

13. Be Wary of Exaggeration:

- Be wary of investment opportunities that guarantee quick success or seem unreal. Something is probably true if it seems too good to be true.

14. Keep Up With Taxes: - Recognise how taxes may affect your overall returns and the tax implications of your investments.

15. Avoid Groupthink:

- Don't heedlessly follow the herd. Your goals and research should guide your investment decisions, not what other people are doing.

16. Keep Current With Regulatory Changes:

- Pay attention to any changes in the law that may affect your investments. Regulations may alter the investing environment and necessitate changing your approach.

17. Steer clear of market timing:

- It is notoriously difficult to time the market by attempting to buy low and sell high. Instead, put your attention on a long-term investment plan.

Making informed investment decisions and staying informed are ongoing processes that call for diligence and research. You will be better able to make decisions that are in line with your financial goals and risk tolerance the more information and understanding you have.

CONCLUSION

In conclusion, the world of finance and investing is constantly changing, so it's important to stay informed and make wise choices if you want to be financially successful. The fundamentals of making an informed decision apply whether you're thinking about making investments in established asset classes like stocks and bonds or more recent asset classes like cryptocurrencies like Bitcoin.